DATE DUE

SEP 0 5 2007	
NOV 1 1 2007	

DEMCO, INC. 38-2931

Moments of Grace

Other books by
Neale Donald Walsch

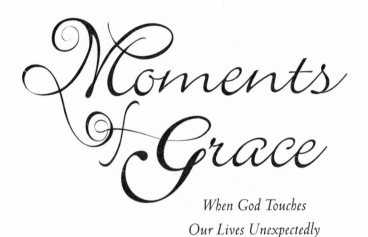

Moments of Grace

When God Touches
Our Lives Unexpectedly

NEALE DONALD WALSCH

HAMPTON ROADS
PUBLISHING COMPANY, INC.

Cover design by Marjoram Productions
Digital imagery © copyright 2001 PhotoDisc, Inc.
For information write:

Hampton Roads Publishing Company, Inc.
1125 Stoney Ridge Road
Charlottesville, VA 22902

Or call: 804-296-2772
Fax: 804-296-5096
e-mail: hrpc@hrpub.com
www.hrpub.com

If you are unable to order this book from your local
bookseller, you may order directly from the publisher.
Call 1-800-766-8009, toll-free.

Library of Congress Catalog Card Number: 00-102567

ISBN 1-57174-303-0

10 9 8 7 6 5 4 3 2 1

Printed on acid-free paper in the United States

*There are more things in Heaven and Earth,
Horatio, than are dreamt of in your philosophy.*

—William Shakespeare

Dedication

For you, Mom.

Acknowledgments

I begin by acknowledging my best friend, God. He's really been great lately. Well, always, really, but lately I've been paying a lot more attention, and so I'm seeing more. Thanks, God. You're tops.

Actually, that is exactly what You are. . . .

Then I want to thank my wonderful wife, Nancy. She's as close to God as I'll ever get in any physical way during this life of mine. Nancy is proof of angels. Someday I'm going to write a book about Nancy, just for myself, and I'm going to call it *Proof of Angels*. Nancy's guiding hand, and her editorial genius, is all over this book.

My deep appreciation goes to Rita Curtis, a good and steady friend, who edited the personal stories in this book after reading hundreds of submissions, and whose extraordinary commitment to the project is absolutely what made it possible.

I honor, too, here on this page my publisher, Robert Friedman, who never waivers when God says, "Okay, Bob, we've got another assignment here. . . ." Bob Friedman and his Hampton Roads Publishing Company are an author's dream.

Table of Contents

Moments of Grace

Introduction

"Is God dead?"

Back in the 1960s that was the big question. Everyone was asking it. People were talking about it. Bumper stickers appeared all over the place with it. It became sort of a catch phrase, a cultural phenomenon. No one seriously thought that God was dead, of course. It was just an interesting way to give ourselves permission as a society to talk about what role—if any—God was playing in our lives.

Along with other slogans, like "Make Love, Not War" and "Try Peace," the three-word God slogan encapsulated the mood of a generation of searchers, mostly young people with shoulder-length hair (male and female) who often wore nothing but beads (sometimes in public) and who couldn't understand what all the fuss was about, and why all the complex questions of life couldn't be, like, answered, man, with a hug. You know, pick flowers, not fights.

The funny thing about it was, they were right.

We *could* solve everything with a hug.

Now we've left the 1900s and we're into the 2000s, and

we're still trying to figure out a way to do that. How can we hug each other when we don't even know each other, when there's such distance between us? We can't even hug ourselves, for goodness sake—and for the same reason. And we're not allowed to *try* to give ourselves and each other love. That's sappy. That's old. That's . . . well, that was for the hippies. We've grown up here. So let's just get on with our lives, right? Do our jobs, pay our bills, meet our obligations, keep our promises, make our peace, and create as few problems as possible on our way out. Okay? I mean, let's not give the matrix any trouble here. Can we just do that, and stop all the nonsense?

Well, I've still got to ask my sixties questions. Where is love in all of this? And where does God fit in?

From the look of things, we're still trying to figure that one out. As a society, as a world, we're still trying to figure that one out.

I'm going to propose a place to start. Let's start by hugging.

This book is a big hug for God. It's kind of like a tip of the hat, a thank you note. No, no . . . a love note. I hope that when you're finished reading this book, you're going to feel as though God has just hugged you, too. Because you know what? God hugs back.

When we hug God, God hugs back.

Oh, heck—God hugs *first*.

That's really what this book is saying. This book is about moments in our lives when God steps in and gives us a great big hug. Those hugs come in many forms, and you'll see a lot of them represented here. Immediately answered requests, "signs" from the heavens, things magically falling into place—all of it. It's all here.

These are stories about real life and real people. Folks sent them to me. Because I asked them to. I wanted to know if my experience of God was really so different from everyone else's, or if, as I suspected, we all are having pretty much the same experience, but I'm the only one who's talking about it. Or one of the very few.

Until now.

I'm happy to say that my *Conversations with God* books have created a conversation *about* God. Even people who disagree with what they've found in those books are at least getting in touch with their own truth about the Divine. And that's good. It's like that old *Is God dead?* question. It's at least given us permission to look at the subject.

And now, here in this collection, people are sharing their own experience of God working in their lives. And I've surrounded these stories with commentaries and reflections based on the rich material in the 1,500 pages of the five *With God* books.

I've made a lot of references to those books, because I think there are some wonderful, and useful, messages there, and I'm hoping to show through these stories how those messages apply to everyday life in a practical way.

So I hope you enjoy this little journey. We're going to learn here all about miracles, and how they can be produced in *your* life. We're going to hear, not from me, but in the stories of other people, a little about God's magic. About incredible synchronicities, about visits by divine voices, about extraordinarily coincidental circumstances, and chance utterances of children that bring wisdom straight from God, and spontaneous events that defy explanation—unless you accept the only explanation there can be.

God did it.

Nope, God is not dead.

Here's proof.

1

When Life Changes Course

Moments of Grace are those times when God intervenes in our lives in very real, very direct, and very visible ways. They are moments when something happens, big or small, that causes a Course Change.

You experienced a Moment of Grace when you picked up this book.

There are many ways that The Divine moves in our lives, especially when we open to the possibility of miracles. Once we have unlocked the door in our psyche to the potentiality of being touched by God in ways we could only imagine in our dreams, then those dreams begin to come true.

A few years ago I wrote a book called *Conversations with God*, which captured attention throughout the world. I believe that book was directly inspired by God during Moments of Grace. And I am very clear that I am not the only one receiving such inspirations and experiencing such moments. For if *Conversations with God* taught us anything, it is that God talks to all of us, all of the time. Yet we can hear God only when we are open to listening.

Let those who have ears to hear, listen.

But now here is the startling news. God not only has conversations with us, God *visits* us every day, *in person*.

This book is all about such visits. It will create a course change in your life because it is about real people, just like you. It is not the story of masters or gurus or saints or sages, but about ordinary folks who have had a "run-in with God"— and never forgot it. Because it is about real people living lives just like yours and mine, it is very convincing on the question of whether there is another force at work in our lives.

In my own mind, that force is called God. You may call it anything you wish. Whatever you call it—coincidence, serendipity, synchronicity, luck, intuition, inspiration—you will find it very difficult, after reading this book, to deny that *it is there*. Right *there*. In our lives. Every day. Working miracles. Making magic. Changing everything.

It happens in everyone's life. Janice Tooke, 43, of Herkimer, New York, says it happened in her life this way . . .

My eleven-year-old son and I were on our way down-state to camp and sail on the Hudson River. During the two-hour drive, we listened, as we always do when we are in the car together, to *Conversations with God*.

On this warm, sunshine-filled August afternoon, we noted that we had seen many, many monarch butterflies during our trip. Feeling full of light and love as we sailed lazily along, I envisioned Jesus in my mind, standing in a field, arms outstretched, calling forth many butterflies. They came as bidden, orange and black and beautiful, and covered him fully, alighting on his arms, his hands, and his head. It was a beautiful image, and it brought calmness to my heart.

Feeling in that moment that I was one with God, I also imagined myself calling forth the butterflies in much the same manner. It was a beautiful moment in my mind. I wanted it to continue. I wanted it to never end.

Then my human doubts crept in. Maybe I'm making it

all up, I thought. All these feelings and visions are nothing but creations of my own imagination. I felt frustrated. I wished there was some way that I could *know* that God is real, and that I am part of Him.

At that moment, I asked God to show me a sign and reveal Himself to me in a tangible way during this trip. I didn't want to have to wait any longer. I wanted it to happen during *this trip*, right here, right now. I even used "I Am" words to call it forth. I said, "*I Am* going to be given a sign."

That evening we camped on an island. The next morning brought a beautiful sunrise to the river. The sunshine sparkled off the water into my eyes as I shook myself awake. While I sat at the picnic table watching waves on the beach, a large monarch butterfly swooped down out of nowhere and began dancing in front of my face. It startled me as it circled once around the top of the tent in which my son was still sleeping.

I immediately said, "Oh, how beautiful you are. Come and see me!" Reaching out my hand, I watched, astonished, as the butterfly alit there!

It was so beautiful! Its orange-and-black wings were huge and perfect, and it sat still for several seconds there in the palm of my hand. My son awoke hearing my voice, and, sticking his head out of the tent, saw the butterfly on my hand.

We were both amazed.

Of course, *I knew who sent this gift*. I have the knowing because I called it forth. And I know that I *can* call it forth, and that we all can, in moments of gratitude and praise and pure at-one-ment with All That Is.

Now, if you're not careful, you could look right past the magnificence of that moment. Or you could agree that it was kind of neat, but that it proved nothing, and that Janice is stretching things to say that it did.

But what would you tell Bill Colson, of Lehi, Utah?

My father's breathing had become difficult, labored.

He'd been lingering between life and death for days. The whole family was there, keeping the vigil.

Wracked by cancer, Dad's weakened body—which seemed to be disappearing right in front of our eyes—shook now and then with what I could only assume were spasms of pain. He'd gone past any ability to complain about it, not having spoken a word, nor opened his eyes, in seventy-two hours.

"My God," my mother said softly at one point, sitting at the side of his bed, "how long can this go on?"

It was after one o'clock in the morning, and the poor dear was exhausted. We all were. But they'd been married sixty-one years. Nothing and no one was going to take Mom away from that bedside now.

That's when I had my conversation with God.

"Must he suffer like this?" I asked Him, silently, urgently, in my heart. "He's been a good man, God. And he's finished his work here. There's nothing left undone, there's nothing more to complete. Please. Won't You take him now? Won't You stop his pain? If You're here, God—*and I know You are*—please, let this end."

At that instant, Dad's breathing became less labored. Within three minutes he slipped away. Gently. Like falling into a deeper sleep.

My eyes filled with tears. I never doubted God before. I'll certainly never even *think* of doubting Him now.

Coincidence? Synchronicity? I don't think so.

A Moment of Grace? Yes.

Moments of Grace are those times when God intervenes in our lives in very real, very direct, and very visible ways. They are moments when something happens, big or small, that causes a Course Change.

You experienced a Moment of Grace when you picked up this book.

2

There Are Many Mansions

Bill Tucker learned the lesson of faith thirty years ago, a lesson he has never forgotten. He has called upon it many times to remind himself that nothing is impossible. Only one thing is required. Belief.

In those days Bill had never sold a house, although he had an agent's license and managed a real estate office. He would often stay late in the evenings to be available to the agents coming in from their evening showings. It was his responsibility to review the offers to purchase, and he didn't want to hold up any deals—or lose any—by not being available on the spot.

Ten o'clock, however, was late enough for any office to be open, he decided one night as he glanced at his watch and yawned. I'm heading home, he told himself. I'm calling it a night. But then he heard voices coming from the front of the office. I must have forgotten to lock the door, he told himself as he rose to investigate.

"I'm sorry," he apologized to the young couple he found standing at the counter, "the office is closed." They were a diminutive pair—she barely five feet tall and he only slightly higher. Two small children hovered shyly behind them.

"Well, the lights are on," the small woman observed. "And you're here, aren't you?" she added sweetly.

"Yes," Bill answered, "but, you see, I'm the manager, not an agent. I'm just waiting for the agents to return so that I can close up for the night."

"We're the Johnsons . . . Ted and Amy. We need to buy a home tonight, so you will have to help us," she insisted.

"Why tonight, Mrs. Johnson?" Bill asked.

She took a breath. "Because we have to move in tomorrow."

It was all Bill could do to stop from rolling his eyes.

"That's impossible, madam," he smiled patiently. "First of all, even if you were to find a house you like at this time of night, we would have to submit an offer to the owner. Then we'd have to wait for a possible counter offer. After that, you have to apply to the bank for a mortgage. The house has to be appraised, and the bank must qualify you. There is absolutely no way you can move into a house in less than six weeks."

There, that should explain it adequately enough, he thought. People never failed to amaze Bill. He chuckled inwardly. Did she actually think she could march in here at ten o'clock at night and get anywhere with this ridiculous notion?

He opened his mouth to suggest that perhaps she should come back tomorrow so that he could introduce her to an agent who might be able to help her, but Mrs. Johnson apparently had other ideas.

"Oh, it won't be any problem at all. We'll be able to buy a house tonight," she said.

Okay, Bill thought. Maybe they have the cash for a house. That, of course, would certainly expedite the process. "Oh? Why is that?" he asked politely in response.

"Because I asked God to give us a home by morning, and He never lets me down."

"I see. Well, even if I had an agent available, it's way too late tonight to look at anything."

She didn't seem to get his point. "You are licensed, aren't you?" she persisted.

Bill answered that he was. "But I've never sold a home and am not expert enough at this for you to trust."

"You believe in God, don't you?"

Bill smiled indulgently. "Sure. On that issue there's no question. But . . . "

She interrupted, "Do you believe in miracles?"

"Well . . . yes." Bill had, in fact, experienced many of what he considered to be amazing occurrences in his life.

Mrs. Johnson drew herself up, stuck out her chest, and said, "Look. I prayed today and asked God to give me a home . . . um, could we just sit down?" Bill nodded, pointing to a couple of seats in front of an agent's desk. He sat in the chair behind it. "I asked God," the woman went on, "to give us a home that we could move into by morning."

Bill's eyebrows shot up.

"We have nowhere to live," Mrs. Johnson said simply. "We thought we'd bought a house on contract from a little old lady here in the city that agreed to finance it for us. We're from about two hundred miles north, but my husband just found a job here, so we packed up and moved. When we arrived, the lady wasn't out yet . . . and when we asked her when she would be leaving, she said she wasn't going to be leaving. She thought she was making a deal with us to live with her. So, she's put us up in her basement."

Bill whistled softly, shaking his head. "That's a very strange tale," he offered. In his twenty years in business he'd heard lots of horror stories, and this one qualified for a place near the top of the list.

Mrs. Johnson continued, "Of course, we can't live in this lady's basement. We have our children here. We've been washing daily at the gas-station restroom down the street.

Tonight I asked God for a miracle because we can't go on like this. So we've been driving around looking for an open real-estate office. And here you are!"

Through the front window Bill could see the couple's old, beat-up car in the parking lot. "How much money do you have for a down payment?" He almost didn't want to hear the answer.

"Oh, we don't have any money at all. Ted has been unable to work for the past ten years. You see, he's a recovering alcoholic and we're getting a new start, but it's not easy. I've been working part-time as a waitress."

This situation is getting worse, Bill thought. How in the world do they think they can buy a home with no money?

"You've been supporting your family on a waitress's salary? Why were you only working part-time?" Bill wondered aloud.

"I had to," Mrs. Johnson explained, "in order to volunteer at my church. That's important to me. But we get by . . . that's not the problem. The problem is, we have nowhere to live. And you know, we're not picky. We'll take the least expensive house we can find."

"Why not just find some place to rent?" Bill suggested. "Get back on your feet, pull some money together, and save for a place."

"We've been renting for years," the woman dismissed. "It's time we had a place of our own. And we can, with God's help. Look how he brought us to you!"

Yeah, well, good luck, lady, Bill thought. At the same time, he was intrigued by the strong faith this woman was exhibiting. And, he mused, who was he to interfere with her miracle? He took out his multiple-listings book. Might as well at least see what there is to see, he told himself with an inward sigh.

"Well, here's one for $54,000. It's not in the nicest part of town, but it's a pretty low price. How much will your husband be making in his new job?"

Mr. Johnson had been quiet up to this point, but now he spoke up.

"I'm darned lucky to have a job at all. I'm starting as a janitor tomorrow, making six bucks an hour."

Bill looked askance at both of them. "That's not much," he observed. Getting out his calculator, he punched in a few numbers. "Less than $12,500 a year."

The man nodded.

Bill said, "The most you can afford on that salary is a $36,000 house. There just aren't any houses in that price range. And even if there were, the bank is going to require a down payment. All this is very unlikely, Mr. and Mrs. Johnson."

"But, you said you believed in miracles," Mrs. Johnson said quietly.

"Yes," Bill smiled meekly, "but I didn't say I could perform them."

The couple only stared at him. Okay, he thought. I'll just have to prove how impossible this is going to be. He picked up the phone and dialed the realtor listing the house he'd just talked about. "We'll make an offer," he said, but he already knew what the outcome would be.

The realtor was delighted with the call at first. Bill saw from the listings book that the house had been on the market for over a year, so he expected this reaction. But when the realtor heard that the offer was $36,000, Bill got the second reaction he'd expected. She became indignant. Bill had to insist that she convey the offer to the owner, reminding her of the law stating that all bona fide offers must be presented.

A few moments later, the realtor called back. "The owner has a counter offer," she said, less annoyed now that at least some kind of deal seemed possible. "It's a good one. Forty-five thousand dollars. I think you should take it."

"Thank you," Bill replied sincerely. "But let me explain the situation here. My clients have no money put aside, and they earn no money to speak of. They'll be lucky to find a bank that will loan them the thirty-six thousand, much less forty-five. We'll keep the negotiations going with a reply of $36,500."

"I'm sure my owner won't accept that," the woman realtor said matter-of-factly.

Bill replied, "You don't have the right to make that assessment. You're required to present our counter-counter offer." He was starting to get into the spirit of things. This might be an interesting exercise, after all.

The realtor rang back in five minutes. "I've made the offer and the owners are willing to have me show the house. We think that when the buyers see it, they'll want to meet our price."

"I don't think they can," Bill told her again.

"I've seen stranger things happen," the selling realtor said. "Let's show the house."

"Okaaay," Bill agreed, and said goodbye. He told the Johnsons what was up. They just sat there, smiling. Bill could hardly believe they'd gotten this far. Of course, in the morning they would all understand the futility of this exercise, but that was part of the real-estate business. They were nice people, and he was willing to go through the process with them until they got the picture.

The next morning as Bill drove to the house, he was unhappily imagining what it would most probably look like. It was, after all, the cheapest house on the market and in the very worst part of town. The street was full of potholes. Abandoned cars and unkempt lawns were everywhere. Bill sighed as he pulled up to a modest front gate.

The selling realtor was waiting for him, the Johnsons standing with her, looking hopeful. He dreaded how sad they were going to be. Bill was glad his job didn't usually entail selling houses and having to sometimes be the instrument of people's disappointment.

As the realtor swung open the gate, Bill caught his breath. The little house was lovely! Mr. and Mrs. Johnson smiled broadly. It was an adorable red-and-white Cape Cod, complete with dormers and shutters on all the windows. When they entered through the front door, Bill noted new carpet and linoleum. All the woodwork had been stripped and stained, there were new appliances and brand new cabinetry in the tiny kitchen. The house was immaculate and fully decorated with new furniture, which would be going with this house, in all the rooms. It was a jewel!

"We'll take it!" Mrs. Johnson blurted happily.

"Great. Let's drive over to the owner's home and conclude the negotiations," the realtor beamed.

The little party caravanned its way out of the slum-like neighborhood into a lovely suburb, pulling up before a spacious ranch. The troupe was met at the front door by a bear of a man dressed in overalls. "Good day to you. I'm George Rockwell," he greeted them warmly, and led them into a cheery kitchen where his wife was pouring coffee for everyone.

When they were settled in chairs, Mr. Rockwell looked Mr. Johnson square in the eye. "What's the matter with you, mister? Why aren't you willing to provide at least the minimum basic house for your family at a reasonable price?"

"Well, sir," started Mr. Johnson, looking down at his cup, "I am willing. My realtor here says I just can't afford any more." He was having difficulty with Rockwell's confrontive approach. "You see," he went on, "I am a recovering alcoholic. I've been unemployed for the last ten years. But I'm sober now, and I just got a new job over at the Harnischfeger Plant."

Mr. Rockwell looked surprised. "Harnischfeger! Who hired you over there?"

"A nice fella by the name of Rogers. Charley Rogers."

Rockwell stood up and extended his hand. "You can have the house for $36,500!"

Bill almost choked on his coffee. "Excuse me," he interrupted as soon as he caught his breath. "We're not even sure we can find a bank to give them a loan."

"No problem," came the answer, "I'll finance it myself."

"Mr. Rockwell," Bill continued, "this buyer hasn't even been qualified."

"Just who are you representing, Mr. Tucker?" the owner of the house now asked. Then his voice softened. "Look, I just retired from Harnischfeger's maintenance department after thirty-six years. Charley Rogers came to me fifteen years ago, a reformed alcoholic. I took a chance on him, and he worked out just fine. If this man's good enough for Charley, he's good enough for me. I am giving him the house for his price right here and now!"

Now the two realtors looked at each other in disbelief. Second cups of coffee were offered all around, and Rockwell began telling the story of the house that was soon to belong to Mr. and Mrs. Johnson—a house, it turned out, that was very dear to his heart.

His father had built the home, and George Rockwell lived his entire life there, marrying and eventually raising his own family in the dwelling. He'd done all the remodeling work himself. His wife had picked out the carpet and the new furniture. The only reason he and Mrs. Rockwell felt compelled to finally move was that they wanted to invest their money in something a little more substantial, something that would produce a greater return down the line, since their son, who suffered from Down's syndrome, would have ongoing financial needs even after their death.

The Johnsons were glowing now, and as the morning sun poured through the windows, Bill felt a little tear squeeze from the corner of his eye even as he noticed the selling realtor dabbing at her mascara.

"Can we move in today?" Amy Johnson inquired hopefully.

Rockwell reached into the pocket of his overalls and pulled out a set of keys. "Be my guest!" he grinned, and put them in Mrs. Johnson's hand.

She looked over at Bill and winked. He winked back. So this is what selling homes—and what life—is about, he thought. Just one miracle after another.

There are many wonderful messages in *Conversations with God*, but none of them more important than this single sentence:

Life proceeds out of your intentions for it.

This reminder from *CWG* helps us to understand the relationship between ourselves and God, and the process of life itself.

Life is not a process of discovery, as in "let's see what happens." Life is a process of creation, as in "let's *choose* what happens."

We have been told that we are made in the image and likeness of God. Well, God is *The Creator*. God creates. So if we truly *are* made in the image and likeness of God, then we, too, must be creators.

This is precisely true. The question is, what is the process by which we create? And the answer is: Through our intentions.

It is by being clear about our intentions that we "help God." Through this device we join with God in acts of conscious cocreation. We use the *power* of God, *consciously*, to produce a specific result.

The story of Mr. and Mrs. Johnson graphically illustrates that. Yet the question this story raises in the mind of those who think about it deeply is, which came first, the chicken or the egg? That is, was it Mrs. Johnson's firm faith in miracles that *produced* the miracle? Or was the miracle already in place *before* she believed in it, or even thought about it, and all she had to do was *see it there*?

What produced the miracle?

That is the question.

Conversations with God tells us that it was Mrs. Johnson's *intentions* that allowed her to experience this particular outcome, as opposed to any one of a number of other possible outcomes.

Could this be true? If so, how does that work?

That is the question Thinking Theology asks. Thinking Theology is a name that I have given to that form of theology which seeks to understand *how* things happen, not just *why* things happen.

For some, it is sufficient to know that *why* Mrs. Johnson got to buy a house in one day is because she had *faith*. For others, there is a deeper inquiry. How does faith *work*? Just exactly *how* does it produce the desired result?

Conversations with God has become such an enormously popular book, translated into twenty-seven languages and read by millions around the world, because it explains—perhaps for the first time in ways that the average person can understand—the How of Life.

And all the *With God* books that have followed, including *Friendship with God* and *Communion with God*, have expanded upon and elaborated this theme, so that now we know the *mechanism* by which God enters our lives, wonders to perform.

And these times of God's entering are what I have called Moments of Grace.

Of course, in the strictest sense, God does not really "enter our lives." If that were true, then it would follow that there were times when God was *not* in our lives. And that is *not* true. It is not true for the simple reason that it is not possible. The only way that it would be possible would be if God and we were separate from each other. If God is separate from us, then there could be times when God is "with us" and times when God is not.

What could *cause* Him to be "with us" or "not with us" could then be the subject of entire religions and complete faith systems. We could devote lifetimes and many books to the basic question, what brings God into our lives?

But what if God was already in our lives? What if God never *left?* What if God could not leave if She wanted to, because God and we are One? What if *that* were true?

Among other things, it would raise a whole different basic question. Not what could bring God into our lives, but *what are we going to do with Him now that we finally see that She's always been there?*

It is in this way that *Conversations with God* upsets the apple cart. By turning the question upside down, we wind up getting entirely different answers.

If God and Mrs. Johnson are One, then it is not a case of Mrs. Johnson asking God to find her a home in one day. Rather, it is a case of Mrs. Johnson *calling forth* that result.

This is done through the mechanism of intention.

Can anyone doubt that it was Mrs. Johnson's *intention* to find and get into a home in twenty-four hours, regardless of what anyone else said was possible or not possible?

Many people have watched their life dreams come to an end because they have not understood what has just been written here. They have accepted what someone else has said is possible or not possible. They have witnessed the termination of their dreams. Yet setting a firm intention can *reverse* that process of termination, through a miraculous reverse process that I call *de-termination.*

De-termination, in effect, "ends the ending." It puts a stop to the stopping. It concludes the concluding, and allows everyone to start over, to begin anew. In some Christian circles this is termed being born again. *Conversations with God* calls this the miracle of recreation, in which we recreate ourselves anew in the next grandest version of the greatest vision ever we held about Who We Are.

Never underestimate the power of determination. That is the reminder we are given through the story of Bill Tucker and the Johnsons.

3

Taken for a Ride

David Daniel is an ardent poker player, so he knows about probabilities. The experience he had as a college student back in the early seventies taught him at a visceral level just how unlikely it is that something called "coincidence" exists.

David was about to begin his freshman year at the University of Southern California. A member of the Resident Honors Program with a major in International Relations, he had been invited to spend a year studying at the University of Tunis, located in the capital of Tunisia in North Africa. It promised to be quite an adventure.

David's parents had encouraged him to spend some time traveling around Europe before starting the school year in mid-September. Still, they were understandably worried. David was just nineteen. His plans called for him to fly to Paris, then travel around France for a while before moving on to Tunisia.

David himself, though naturally excited, was a bit on edge about the trip. Here he was not yet twenty and he was about to be making his own way in a totally foreign culture.

Hmmm, he thought, this could be a real learning experience . . . or quite a disaster.

When the ponytailed young man in patched jeans arrived at Kennedy Airport with a pack on his back, he was long on eagerness and short on experience in being *anywhere* away from home. *Would it go well?* he wondered. *My God, Paris!* he mused. *And Tunisia! What am I going to do when I get there? I can't even speak the language! And I don't know anybody.*

A little unnerved by his own last-minute jitters, David found himself wandering around the airport, trying to keep his mind off of what could go wrong. And because his schedule had him arriving many hours before his late-night flight overseas, he had plenty of time to worry.

Finally, he decided to ride into Manhattan to spend some of that time having a look around. Wanting to save his money for Europe, he thought about hitchhiking. He'd never been to New York. It would be a good afternoon's adventure, he told himself, and it should be a snap getting a ride outside the airport.

Wrong.

Cars whizzed by, ignoring his stuck-out thumb. *Man, I can't even make my way around New York*, David berated himself. *How do I think I'm going to make it in France?*

He was about to abandon his idea about Manhattan when a vehicle slowed to a crawl and stopped in front of him.

"Where are you headed, son?" asked the pleasant man behind the wheel.

"Into Manhattan," David replied hopefully. "Thought I'd look around a bit before I fly out to Paris tonight."

"Well, I'm not going to Manhattan, but I can take you part of the way, then let you off where you can get a ride on into town."

Delighted, David jumped in. Things have taken a turn for the better, he grinned to himself.

Wrong.

David was surprised when his host pulled over behind an island in the middle of a freeway system and motioned for him to get out. "What's up?" he asked nervously.

"This is as far as I can take you," the driver said, then, responding to David's dumbfounded expression, "I told you I wouldn't be going all the way."

There were at least four exit options converging at this one place, all going in different directions to different parts of the city. David had no idea where he was, or how to get to where he wanted to go. And in his state of sudden paralysis, he did not even have the presence of mind to ask the driver! He could only hear, "Son, you have to get out." He thanked the man for the ride and stepped onto the island in the middle of the highway.

Now despair overcame David as he looked out at the rush-hour traffic zooming by. *I'll* never *get a ride here*, he thought hopelessly.

Even if someone *were* to actually stop, and that was highly unlikely, that person would have to be going to Manhattan, and not to any of the other exit choices! And walking to a more convenient place, or even back to the airport, was not an option. He was smack in the middle of several freeways, and, he muttered to himself, in quite a mess.

David shifted the backpack on his shoulder and stuck out his thumb in resignation.

Hundreds of cars passed. An hour went by . . . then another. David watched the faces of the drivers as they intently made their way to their destinations. Hardly anyone even noticed him, and when someone did, it was with a puzzled look or, worse, with amusement. And David figured he knew just what those people were thinking.

"Does this kid really imagine that he's going to get a ride out *here?*"

David couldn't help but agree. His prospects, he assessed, looked pretty bleak.

Strategizing about what he would do in case no one stopped for him, *ever*, he decided that when the rush hour was over he would traverse the crisscrossing roads and make his way to a bus stop somewhere. He began to worry. If something didn't happen soon, there would be no time left to go into Manhattan. He would have to get back to the air-port to catch his plane to Paris—and he would be lucky to make his late-night flight.

Now his thinking really started to turn negative. You know, I'm pretty exposed out here, he began thinking to himself. Anything could happen. And even if a police car stops, I may be safe, but I may also be in trouble. Hitchhiking isn't allowed on freeways. I might be held by the police and then miss my plane . . .

In the midst of mulling over these dark notions, David stopped himself. *Wait a minute, this is crazy! Nothing bad is going to happen.* He shook his head at himself. *I've got to think positively here.*

A few minutes later he noticed a late-model station wagon slowing a little, the driver looking over with concern. Then he watched with incredulity as the car actually pulled over! The driver motioned to David to get in.

"Thank you, thank you, *thank you*," David repeated under his breath as he grabbed his backpack and ran to the open door.

"Going to Manhattan?" David asked right away. He now knew that this was an important question to have answered before the car took off. He didn't want to find himself on yet another island in the midst of another impossible knot of highways!

The driver looked over at David with deep brown eyes. "Yes, Manhattan," he answered with a soft accent. They drove for a half-mile or so before they spoke again. David asked him, "Where are you from?"

"I am from Tunisia. In North Africa."

What? If David could have slammed on the brakes, he would have. "You're from T-Tunisia?" he stammered.

"Yes, but it's been a while since I have been home. I actually lived in Paris for the past few years, and have just this month moved to New York. I practice medicine in Manhattan."

"You lived in Paris? You're from Tunisia and you've been living in Paris?"

David couldn't believe his ears. "*I'm* on my way to Tunisia, and I'm stopping over in Paris for a month!"

The man's eyes widened and his face broke into a smile. "Well, then it looks like I've chosen the right passenger. Perhaps I can help you in your travels."

For the forty-five-minute drive to Manhattan, David and the doctor engaged in a sprightly discussion about all the people and places that would be a part of David's life for the next year. The driver gave David the names of a few close friends and of several acquaintances. They could tell him about the best places to go and things to see, the out-of-the-way restaurants and galleries, possible apartments to rent, people to meet—all the things David would need to know to make his visit to France enjoyable and beyond what a mere tourist would have available to him.

The very next day, shortly after landing at Charles de Gaulle International Airport, David began reaping the benefits of his ride into Manhattan. He ended up actually being invited to live in the spare bedroom of a couple whose name and phone number in Paris had been given him on the ride to Manhattan that day.

A few weeks later, the Tunisia contacts given to him allowed David to become acquainted with the university, becoming comfortable in that faraway city with a very different culture much sooner than he ever thought possible. He was finding places to frequent and to live and work while he was a student, so he had few real worries. His whole experience went well.

Yet David's life—his sense of confidence, the future opportunities which rolled out of that experience—might have been . . . no, *would* have been . . . totally different had this kind man, this *particular* man, not stopped for a desperate hippie thumbing a ride in the middle of the freeway on a summer morning in New York.

David never saw his benefactor again. For weeks he wrote letters to thank the man for his kind introductions, but they were never answered. Eventually, David realized that the chance meeting had served a higher purpose in his life, and there was little need to pursue the doctor further. The important encounter had taken place, and had set the course of David's year as a student abroad.

These days David tells this story a lot. Some people make light of the cosmic context in which David frames it. But none have failed to be awed by the sheer synchronicity of what occurred on that highway.

"The way that it has served me the most," David says, "other than the obvious gift of making my travels far more enjoyable, is that it showed me unequivocally that there are moments in life in which wonders occur, and these are not to be left unnoticed or unexamined.

"There is a purpose and a meaning in everything. We have the unique opportunity to pay attention—or not—and thus chart the course of our lives."

I picked up a wonderful piece of wisdom a few years ago from Werner Erhard. Werner, an extraordinary teacher who created the *est* trainings, said: "Life works out in the process of Life itself."

Those are nine of the most comforting words I have ever heard. They've allowed me to *relax* about life and give it a chance.

My own rearticulation of this wisdom comes out as five words.

God is on our side.

I believe this firmly and fully. It is the basis of an entire book, *Friendship with God*, which I produced in 1999. It is the basis of my entire philosophy and understanding of life.

I believe that God demonstrates His "on-our-side-ness" every minute of every day—and some days in more dramatic ways than others. The story of David Daniel is a powerful example.

I believe that all of us have stories like this. I believe all of us can point to moments in our lives of astonishing synchronicity, serendipity, coincidence, luck, or whatever we choose to call them. I call them Moments of Grace. They form a particular category of a larger collection of such moments that I see all of us moving through—but only a few of us doing so consciously.

When we do so consciously, recognizing these Moments of Grace for what they really are, something quite remarkable happens. They begin to multiply. This is because the more we know what is happening, the more we know what is happening.

Let me see if I can make that more clear.

Awareness is the key to consciousness, and consciousness is the key to creation. As we become keenly aware, we become ever more keenly aware. Awareness is something that grows, that feeds on itself. After one becomes Aware, one becomes aware that one is Aware. Then, one becomes aware that one is aware that one is Aware, and so on, until we reach the ultimate level of Total Awareness.

When we become Aware that there are such things in life as Moments of Grace, we begin to recognize them very quickly. Recognizing them more quickly allows us to benefit from them more easily. To a casual observer, we may even seem to be creating them. In one sense, we *are* creating them—if we accept the definition of "creation" as the act of seeing something (and thus taking advantage of something) that is already there.

Simply put, we don't have to create anything. We merely have to use to our benefit all that has already been created. *And to know with a certainty that we can do so.*

Now this is where the lines seem to blur. They aren't really blurred, but they may seem to be.

In the case of Mr. and Mrs. Johnson, we said the *intention* is what produces the space for miracles to occur, like finding and buying a house in twenty-four hours with virtually no money. We asked, what produced the miracle? Was the miracle in place before Mrs. Johnson believed in it, or did she, in a sense, *put* it in place through her belief?

Now we are saying here that we "merely have to use to our benefit all that has already been created." This seems to answer the question, suggesting that the miracle was already in place, and all Mrs. Johnson had to do was *see it there*, presumably through her faith.

Yet faith is a tricky thing. It is very difficult for many people to believe something that they "don't believe." If something is "unbelievable," how does a person move to a space of believing it? How does a person "acquire faith"?

My observation is that "faith" is acquired in three ways. By noticing, by experiencing, and by deciding. We can *notice* how things work out for other people (by reading books like this!), we can *experience* how things work out (as David Daniel did), or we can firmly set our *intention* ahead of time about how things are going to work out (the route taken by Mrs. Johnson).

This can, in fact, become a three-part, stair-step process. First, you hear about other people's miracles. Then, through hearing about enough of them, you raise your awareness and begin to notice that you, too, are receiving miracles in *your* life. Finally, through receiving enough of them, you decide that miracles must be pretty commonplace, and you begin to absolutely *expect* them—even *require* them—by setting your intention!

Interestingly, not all of these steps have to be taken. Nor do they have to be taken in that order. One can "leapfrog" a step, or take a step out of sequence.

What occurred for David Daniel on that day when he made his first visit to New York City as a college student was a moment that could "look like" a huge inconvenience, if not disaster. In truth, it was a Moment of Grace, a time of Divine Intervention, from which nothing but benefit would spring.

Its power was not only the outcomes it produced in David's life in the short term, but the *faith* and *knowing* that it put into his life in the long term.

David now knows, and has known since that day when he was very young, that life works out in the process of life itself, that God is on our side. There is no question about this in his mind, because he has had a direct *experience* of it, and he is now clear about the Process of Life and how it works. He went right to Step 2.

The beauty of the "system" is that his clarity produces even more such incidents, even more such results. That is because his insight allows him to see all things differently, and *that* allows him to *experience* things differently. And, to *expect to*. He can now move to Step 3.

But before David's "Miracle of the Hitchhike," he was very worried, wondering how he would get out of his mess. On the other hand, before her Miracle of the House, Mrs. Johnson wasn't worried at all—even though her miracle, too, was yet to come.

What made the difference? *Intention.* Mrs. Johnson moved right to Step 3. We don't have enough of her back story to know whether she leapfrogged to that step or got there through steps 1 and 2. And, of course, it doesn't matter. What matters is that she set her sights and never wavered. She never allowed herself to fall into negative thinking, something that is often very easy to do when things do not look good. She never allowed herself to relax her intention by giving in to what appeared to be happening. By not relaxing her intention, she held everything *in tension.*

Here is a secret of life. Used properly, tension is good. I am talking here about what psychologists call "creative tension." In fact, this is *exactly* what I am talking about: tension which *creates.*

When things are held in creative tension, opposing energy forces are used against each other to hold things in place. This is how you keep things in place when it looks to all the world as if everything is falling apart, that it can't work, that there's no use.

It is when you *release* the tension that everything falls apart. It is when you let go, give up, like children playing tug-of-war, that everything comes tumbling down.

The trick is to stay in tension, until that which opposes you finally lets go. Then things do not fall down, *they fall into place.*

This is exactly what happened to Mr. and Mrs. Johnson.

David Daniel was fortunate that his own downturn in thinking, his turn to negativity out there on that traffic island, was brief, not generating enough negative energy to terminate his dream of getting into Manhattan and back to the airport in time for his flight.

He cut himself off from negative thinking just in time and "stopped the stopping." He stopped stopping himself from receiving his own good. He almost terminated his own good, but he reversed course through the process I have called de-termination.

Lo and behold, a miracle! Out of nowhere not only does someone come along who is going to Manhattan, but it is the most right and perfect person you could imagine for that situation.

David reports today that his life has been "filled with such incidents." This is no doubt true. For what you think, you experience. And if what you think is that the present circumstance—what*ever* it may be—will ultimately bring you to your highest good, there is no doubt that it will.

It can be no other way, for your experience is not something that is happening, it is something that you *think* is happening. That is, it is not something that is "going on," it is something that you *feel* about what is going on!

What you feel about what is going on is what is going in. It is going into your heart, into your soul, and into your mind. It is creating a record in all three, and that record is what you call your *experience*.

Two people can hear the same piece of music and have entirely different experiences of it. It is the same with two people and food, two people and sex, two people and anything.

If, every time you find yourself "in a pickle" (as David seemed to be on that traffic island in the middle of the freeway), you are a*ware* that what is facing you is an opportunity, not an obstacle, you will not fall into negative thinking, and everything about how you experience your circumstance will change.

That is the point.

And the larger point is that you don't even have to know that something good is occurring for it to be occurring. *It is occurring whether you know it or not.* Yet if you wish to *experience* the "good" that is occurring, you must *see it as that.*

This is what awareness is. This is what it means.

The trick in life is to observe—to simply *observe*—what is going on, without judgment. Do not call it one thing or another. *Do not fall into negativity.* Simply become an objective observer.

I have just been dropped off by a driver in the middle of the freeway system of New York City.

In David Daniel's story, that is what was true. Every other thought that David had about that was a judgment.

Fortunately, God doesn't care if we judge things. God will always make sure that everything occurring is to our benefit. The only question, then, is not whether a particular occurrence *is* to our benefit, *but how long it will take for us to notice that.*

The sooner we become aware that *all* things are to our benefit, the sooner we will experience them that way.

Listen to *Conversations with God, Book 2* on this subject:

> Because it is My will that you should know, and experience, Who You Are, I allow you to draw to yourself whatever event or experience you choose to create in order to do that.
>
> Other Players in the Universal Game join you from time to time—either as Brief Encounters, Peripheral Participants, Temporary Teammates, Long-Time Interactors, Relatives and Family, Dearly Loved Ones, or Life Path Partners.
>
> These souls are drawn to you by you. You are drawn to them by them. It is a mutually creative experience, expressing the choices and desires of both.
>
> No one comes to you by accident.
>
> There is no such thing as coincidence.
>
> Nothing occurs at random.
>
> Life is not a product of chance.
>
> Events, like people, are drawn to you, by you, for your own purposes. . . .

When we understand this, we transform our lives. Or, we *appear* to. In truth, all we do is see them for what they really are. Likewise, it is impossible to transform ourselves. It is only possible to know ourselves or to not know ourselves as Who We Really Are. When we do, we transform our *experience*.

I know that life works out in the process of Life Itself. I know that God is on my side. This keeps my creative tension in place. The line between the Positive Me and the Negative Me remains taut, until the Negative Me gets so tired of hanging on that he finally lets go. Then everything that one half of me was insisting could not possibly work out falls right into place!

Now that I know this trick, I experience my life as being worry-free. I see all things leading to good. And this truth has set me free. Free of frustration. Free of anger. Free of anxiety.

If and when I fall back into those experiences, it is because I have forgotten Who I Really Am and What Is So. I have forgotten that life works out in the process of Life Itself. I have forgotten that God is on my side.

I am not paying attention. That is, I am not *at tension*. I have relaxed into negative thinking.

I have forgotten that my ride is on the way, and I imagine that I am on one hell of an island.

4

Miracles Do Happen

Fred Ruth was sitting in his chair waiting to die. He wanted a drink. "I don't need any damn doctor to tell me I'm not hanging around much longer," he grumbled. "Everyone knows I'm next in line."

Just yesterday the cardiologist had made a few phone calls, telling Fred's ex-wife and children that it was time now to visit their father to say goodbye. A couple of his kids had shown up to see him, but they hadn't hung around too long. Fred hadn't been all that civil to them in recent times, especially to his stepson. The two of them hadn't gotten along that well when Fred was feeling well, much less now that he was really sick.

The problem was his heart. It had been bad since 1975 when Fred had his first serious attack. He was only thirty-eight, but it had come as no surprise when it happened. His mother and father had both died of heart attacks, he had lost two brothers to heart disease, and his sister had suffered from serious diabetes and had just died the previous year of a heart attack at age forty-four.

Fred himself had undergone bypass surgery twice in the past six years. He hadn't worked in a long time, but he didn't really miss his job all that much. There was too much stress being a manager in a computer manufacturing company. It had probably exacerbated his heart problems. Good riddance, was all he had to say.

"Turn the volume down," he barked at Anne, who was watching TV. Didn't she understand how sick he was?

Fred knew his own personality had changed, but he didn't seem to be able to do anything about it. He was just turning irritable. Ornery and irritable. And that was that.

"God, how I hate sitting here," Fred grumbled as he attempted to uncurl from his position in the recliner and look out the window. It hurt to move. There was so little oxygen in his blood that all his limbs and his chest were one solid cramp. He rarely moved from the chair; it was all he could do to walk to the bathroom.

Fred's entire world had gradually become this one pie-shaped, three-hundred-square-foot room. He couldn't go outside because the apartment building was two stories, and that meant climbing stairs; he could only watch the world go by outside his window. Every once in a while an ambulance would scream down the street and Fred would wonder if he might be the next one taking that ride.

There was precious little to occupy Fred's mind. He'd lost interest in television; those sitcoms seemed so stupid. Lately he'd been mostly reading Stephen King novels, the only books that could hold his attention anymore. Anne (her full name was Roseanna, but Fred had always fondly used the derivative) had tried to talk to him about some spiritual books she'd been reading, but it all seemed like a bunch of bull to him.

Fred had never been much interested in God or religion, and the fact that he was dying didn't mean he was going to change now. He'd gone to church a few times as a boy, but no one in his family had gone with him, and after a while there didn't seem to be much point. It sure hadn't made his life any better during the time he did go, he thought. Nothing had seemed to make his life better . . . except maybe a drink now and then.

"Would you like something to eat before I go out to my meeting?" Anne asked, coming into the living room wearing her coat.

"What meeting? You didn't tell me you were going to a meeting. I don't want to be alone. And I don't want any food. Just bring me a drink."

"Fred, you shouldn't be drinking. It can't be good for you," Anne said cautiously.

"What's it gonna do, kill me?" was Fred's unkind retort.

It was winter in Ohio. The day had been sunny and cold, but the clouds had come in late in the afternoon and the sky had taken on an ominous look. Fred noticed that the trees were starting to be blown around quite a bit.

"The wind is coming up; there's gonna be a storm. That's another reason you shouldn't be going out tonight."

But Anne had already taken off her coat.

He reached for the remote control, then decided he didn't even have enough energy to use it. As he lay back in his chair, listening to the wind, Fred had no sense of how much time was passing. Soon he heard the television, so he knew Anne was watching it again, but he just sat in his chair with his eyes closed, feeling the pain in his body. There was some thunder, and the wind was blowing pretty hard, but Fred didn't move.

Maybe all this will be over soon, he thought with a sigh. I can't see the point of having to just hang on like this, in all this pain. I wish it were over.

Then it happened. A gigantic *boom,* so loud that it shook the room. Immediately behind his closed eyelids, Fred discerned a flash. When his eyes flew open in surprise he saw before him a bright ball of light the size of a basketball hovering just above the television set.

Fred blinked. The brilliance hurt his eyes, but he felt compelled to look closer. The ball had a fiery orange center with a brilliant white aura shimmering all around it, and a tail, sort of like he imagined a comet might look. Fred couldn't speak. His brain seemed not to be able to take this in. All he could do was stare at the strange, shining ball. Then, it blew up. Right there. Before his eyes. It just . . . *burst*. There was no noise and it was not really an explosion, but it seemed as if the ball blasted tiny particles of light into the room—and into Fred.

Fred felt a surge of energy unlike anything he had ever known enter his chest. He was immediately warm, and his entire body began to tingle.

At that point, Fred found his voice. He looked over at Anne sitting on the couch, her mouth hanging open.

"You saw that, right?" Fred wanted to make sure he wasn't dreaming.

His wife nodded slowly. "Are we dead?"

"I don't know. But if we get up and move across the room and look back at empty chairs, then we'll know we aren't dead." Fred found it odd that he was being humorous at a time like this.

Anne and Fred walked tentatively to the opposite wall and turned around. There were no bodies sitting in their chairs. Fred took a deep breath. "Well, I guess we're still alive. I think I'll go outside and find out if anyone else saw anything."

Before Anne could say a word, Fred had left the apartment, apparently without a second thought. He hurried down the flight of stairs and went outside in the blowing wind. Leaves and limbs scattered the sidewalk. Walking around the block to check for damage to the building, he could hear sirens in the distance. Two men were on the street and Fred walked up to them.

"Some storm, huh?" he said.

"Yeah," one of the men said, then pointed out the darkened windows a couple of blocks from their corner. "Looks like there are some power outages down the way."

Fred thought he should get back upstairs to check on Anne. She was probably pretty darn scared, if she was feeling anything close to what he was feeling. When he walked through the door, he found Anne just standing there, looking not frightened, but shocked.

"Do you know what you just did? Do you realize what you've just done?" She was incredulous.

Fred stopped in his tracks. He looked down at his frail body, then back up at his wife. What had happened to him? Slowly, it dawned on him that he had actually gone down a flight of stairs, walked around the block, and climbed back up the stairs. And he wasn't even winded! Just a few minutes before, he hadn't been able to walk to the bathroom without incredible pain, much less up a flight of stairs. Now he didn't feel one bit of discomfort. In fact, he felt great! What had happened to him?

"I'm going to do it again," he said, not believing any of this. Fred went downstairs and walked around the block twice more. "I feel like a million bucks," he said to Anne when he returned. "The pain is gone."

Fred hasn't experienced any pain since. He called his cardiologist, but when the doctor heard his story, he said he didn't want to talk about it. Then Fred phoned the physician at the local urgent care clinic to which he had been going for pain control.

"Well, Fred, I hear a lot of strange stories like this," the doctor allowed, "and I've learned not to be too surprised. Go out and enjoy your life, and if you have pain again, come back. In the meantime, you don't need my help."

Fred *is* enjoying his life. Something has changed, not just in his body, but also in his personality and in the way he feels about his life. He feels less in need of controlling everyone and everything. He doesn't drink anymore, and his children and friends are coming around more often.

The miracle, as they choose to call it, has brought Anne and Fred close together, too. They are even having long conversations these days about spiritual matters and are sharing and discussing personal-growth books, whose philosophies Fred is now openly integrating into his life.

In an attempt to give something to their community, Fred and Anne have started writing and distributing a local spiritual newsletter to provide a forum for discussions about mind-body-spirit topics. He doesn't ask much anymore why he received this dramatic healing. He is sure that it is because he still had something to give to the world and, in order to do this, he had to be healed in body and spirit.

Anne believes the miracle was for both of them.

Sometimes our Moments of Grace are not so graceful. Sometimes God comes along and gives us a real jolt. And once in a while those "jolts" come in the form of experiences that could only be explained as . . . well, as inexplicable. When this occurs we are left to ponder, what has happened here? What's going on?

In *Friendship with God* there is an extraordinary statement.

"I have given you nothing but miracles."

The message here is that we can expect miracles every day of our lives. But, as with noticing the sudden alighting of a butterfly, we must be aware that they are occurring. Otherwise, we will look right past them.

Unless we don't. Because we can't. Sometimes it's impossible to ignore them. As Fred and Anne Ruth discovered.

Before we explore this wonderful miracle, however, I would like to talk for a very brief moment about some of the reasons that healing miracles may be necessary in the first place.

We are not taking good enough care of ourselves. Not just Fred, most of us.

Conversations with God, Book 1 makes this observation:

All illness is self-created. Even conventional medical doctors are now seeing how people make themselves sick.

Most people do so quite unconsciously. So when they get sick, they don't know what hit them. It feels as though something has befallen them, rather than that they did something to themselves.

This occurs because most people move through life—not simply health issues and consequences—unconsciously.

People smoke and wonder why they get cancer.

People ingest animals and fat and wonder why they get blocked arteries.

People stay angry all their lives and wonder why they get heart attacks.

People compete with other people—mercilessly and under incredible stress—and wonder why they have strokes.

The not-so-obvious truth is that most people worry themselves to death.

And, five books and five years later, in *Communion with God*, we find the following commentary:

Health is an announcement of agreement between your body, mind, and spirit. When you are not healthy, look to see which parts of you disagree. Perhaps it is time for you to rest your body, but your mind does not know how. Perhaps your mind is dwelling on negative, angry thoughts, or worries about tomorrow, and your body cannot relax.

Your body will demonstrate the truth to you. Simply watch it. Notice what it is showing you; listen to what it is saying.

If we listen to our bodies, and treat them well, we will get a great deal more use out of them. The miracle that we can expect every day will be the miracle that we perform.

So now, let's talk about miracles.

A Course in Miracles says that with miracles there are no

degrees of difficulty. This is because, for God, nothing is difficult. All things are possible, and not merely possible, but easy.

Yet while there are no degrees of difficulty, there are different kinds and sizes. There are big miracles and small miracles. There are quick miracles and miracles that take more time. There are miracles that can be easily explained and miracles that cannot.

Not all miracles look like healings. Fred Ruth was healed, but that should not make other people wonder why their loved one didn't get a "miracle" but died. Even a person dying can be a miracle, though it may not be what we might want the miracle to look like.

My definition of a miracle is "just exactly the right thing, in just exactly the right way, at just exactly the right time." The story at the end of chapter 1 of the elder Mr. Colson's departure from his body is a wonderful example. So is, in a less dramatic but no less perfect way, the story of the man who picked up David Daniel standing on that traffic island in the middle of New York City's freeway system.

Whenever I pray for a miracle, for myself or for another, I have found it very strengthening and very comforting to "let God decide" what the miracle will look like. I use these words: "This is what I would like, God, but *only if this is for the highest and best good of all concerned.* Please, God, do what is for the highest and best good. Of everyone. I know you will. Amen."

I have used this prayer for twenty-five years, and it has been so comforting. It is my version of "let go and let God."

I have said before that the more we realize miracles are happening every day in our own lives, the more miracles we will experience occurring. Yet many miracles go ignored, unrecognized for what they are, because they are not considered by us to be "miraculous."

Frequently it is not what has occurred that is miraculous

but the timing of what occurred. The event may be easily explained, but the fact that it happened *when* it happened is what made it unusual. And so, we may not call this a miracle, but rather, *synchronicity*.

Often what is miraculous is not what or when something has happened, but how. A series of totally explainable events may come together in a particular, almost quixotic, way to produce a highly improbable result. We may not call this a miracle, but rather, *serendipity*.

Sometimes the event that is occurring in our lives is totally explainable, and neither its timing, nor even the way it is happening, is unusual. Yet the fact that it is happening *at all*, and *to us*, is overwhelming. Still, we may not even call *this* a miracle, but rather, *luck*.

Many human beings will give every name they can think of to God's miracles except "God's miracle," because they either don't believe in God, or don't believe in miracles—or don't believe that miracles can happen to *them*. And if you don't believe something, you will not see it for what it really is. Because believing is seeing. It is not the other way around.

It is for just this reason that you may not see *yourself* as Who You Really Are. You do not even know your Self to be a miracle. Yet that is what you are. A miracle in the making. For you are not nearly finished with yourself yet, and God is never finished with you.

This is what Fred Ruth learned during the weeks when he thought that he was going to die. God had different plans for Fred, and He tried everything to wake Fred up. He even had Anne bring Fred books and talk to him about spiritual matters. But Fred just wasn't listening. So God said, "Okaaay . . . let's see what we can do to get Fred's attention here. . . ."

Many of us have had these kinds of wake-up calls from the universe. But, as mentioned, we'll label them anything and everything else we can think of.

Psychological aberrations.

Paranormal experiences.

Flights of our imagination.

Whatever. Yet they are miracles nonetheless.

But do these kinds of things really occur? Do people actually see balls of light in front of them, or feel energy beams running through them, or hear gentle voices speaking great truths? Do people truly experience spontaneous healings, or suddenly feel a total Oneness with the universe, or actually have conversations with God?

Uh, yes.

5

The Voiceless Voice

After the publication of *Conversations with God*, the question that I was asked more often than any other was: "Why you? Why did God pick you?"

I can't tell you how many times I've answered that. And, always, I've responded with, "God did *not* pick me. God picks everyone. God is speaking to all of us, all the time. The question is not, to whom does God talk? The question is, who listens?"

God talks to us in many ways every day. God is shameless and will use any device to communicate with us. The lyrics to the next song you hear on the radio. The chance utterance of a friend on the street that you "just happen" to meet. An article in a four-month-old magazine at the hair salon. And, yes, a voice that speaks directly to you.

But you must *listen.* You must be *aware* that God communicates *directly* with you. This is not a hope. This is not a wish. This is not a prayer. This is a *reality.* God's communications come to you in Moments of Grace. But you will move right through those moments, and not even know that they occurred, if you are not *aware.*

I keep making this point, over and over again, because I want you to attune your spiritual self. I want you to open your eyes and ears. I want you to awaken your senses. I want you to "come to your senses" about God! *Because God's messages are coming to you all the time.*

Do you need more examples? Do you need additional proof? Read this next story. It is about Doug Furbush, who lives near Atlanta, Georgia.

Moving into their newly built house had been a dream come true for Doug and his family, and Doug had been putting in long weekend days to get the sprinkler system installed before the winter rains.

It was work he enjoyed—digging in the soil, laying sod. Getting a little dirt under his fingernails was a nice change from sitting in front of a computer all day, which is the way he spent most of his time in his job as a technology consultant.

The September sun warmed his back as he bent over the shovel.

"I'm going to make a quick trip to the supermarket," his wife called from the back door. "Do you need anything?"

"No thanks, honey!" Doug shouted.

"Okay! Back in ten!"

Doug chuckled to himself. I don't need a darn thing in the whole, wide world.

He had just about everything he could possibly want. There seemed to be nothing in his universe at the moment that he would change. Life was good. It was all good—the sun on his shoulders, the thud and crunch of the shovel hitting the soil, the birds warbling from high atop the peach tree in the yard. As he dug, the pleasure of his labor sang in his muscles. Sweat poured between his shoulder blades.

Suddenly, he heard his name called.

Doug.

The tone was urgent, but it was a voice he did not recognize. Almost like . . . a voiceless voice.

He looked around. The yard was empty. Was that his wife? It must have been. Maybe she'd forgotten something and called to him from the driveway. When he didn't respond, she went in to get it herself.

Yeah, that's it.

Pushing the shovel into a mound of dirt, Doug pulled himself up out of the ditch and walked to the front of the house. No one was there. His wife's car was not in the garage.

Hmm. Maybe I've been out in the sun too long, he mused, and headed back toward the yard.

Doug!

The voice was more insistent this time.

Go find Gael!

Now Doug stopped cold in his tracks. *What* is *this? I heard that voice*, he argued with himself. *But where is it coming from? And what's this about Gael?*

His daughter had returned earlier from a morning at the local skating rink with her friends, going directly to her room. She had seemed a little quiet, but Doug had been so busy with his project that he'd hardly spoken to her. She was, after all, thirteen. He smiled to himself. *She's going to have moods.*

But now, a feeling of dread came over him . . . like something was wrong. Why was he hearing this voice urging him to go find her?

All these thoughts took but seconds. Abruptly, Doug bounded into the house, not stopping to remove his mud-caked boots, and took the stairs two-by-two up toward Gael's bedroom.

As usual, the door was locked. This was The Inner Sanctum. Doug understood all about that. But something felt different here. It was not like the other times his daughter had cloistered herself.

"Gael?" he knocked on the door.

Nothing.

Now he pounded harder. "Gael, are you in there? Is something wrong?"

More silence.

"Gael, open the door!"

Then came the small, muffled voice.

"Leave . . . me alone . . . Dad."

Well, at least she was okay, she was speaking. But there was no way that Doug was going to walk away.

"Gael, open this door. *Now.*"

He waited a beat. *I'll have to break it down*, he thought. Then he heard the click of the lock.

Barely opening the door, Gael turned and ran toward her bed, jumping under the blankets and covering her head. Her shaking form betrayed silent sobs.

"What's wrong, honey?" Doug asked, making his way to her. "Did something happen to you?"

The same mumble as before—"Leave me alone, Dad."

Doug's eyes scanned the room in bewilderment, and that's when he saw blood on the coverlet. It was just a spot, but he saw it, and he touched it, and it was damp.

"Gael, talk to me. Have you hurt yourself?"

She did not respond.

"Please, Gael, tell me what's wrong. Why is there blood on your bed?"

His daughter uncovered her face. Her eyes were swollen and red . . . and so were her wrists, Doug saw immediately. She'd cut her wrists.

"Gael, baby, what have you done?" Doug was frantic. He grabbed her arms for a closer look. He saw immediately that she had not done serious damage. The slashes were not deep. But she was bleeding, for sure. Doug raced to the bathroom to find something. "Why did you do this, Gael?" he sent over his shoulder. "What's happened to you?"

Now she sobbed openly. "Daddy, I'm so sorry, but I just can't take it anymore."

"What? Take *what?*"

"Everyone is so mean to me. Everyone hates me."

"Oh, Gael. . . . " Doug interrupted, returning to her bed with towels. "That's not true."

"Please, Dad. You don't know. I have no friends. And the one person I like is so mean to me. One day she likes me, then the next day she hates me and talks about me behind my back."

Her father cleaned her gently with a warm washcloth.

"Today at the skating rink she was so cruel. I just don't think I can take it anymore. Last week she invited me to her birthday party. I was so happy. And today, in front of everyone, she told me she's decided not to invite me after all. I just wanted to die."

"But, Gael, nothing is bad enough to do *this*. You will have friends. There will be lots of birthday parties. You're a nice, beautiful person. There are many people who will want to be friends with you." Doug pleaded with his daughter. "Please, you can't possibly believe that your life isn't worth living. What about us, your parents? We love you very, very much."

At that moment, the front door slammed. "I'm home, guys. Wanna see what I got?" Doug's wife called cheerfully from the foyer. "Helloooo. Where is everybody?"

"There's your Mom. Let's talk to her, okay? She'll want to know what's happening with you." Doug had wrapped Gael's wounds with the towels. "We need to take you for stitches, honey. Come on."

Gael rose reluctantly and slid her feet into her shoes, holding the bloody towels in place around her wrists. Doug looked down at the mud he'd tracked in on the pink carpet. Then he shook off the irrelevant thought. What a dumb thing to worry about, he chastised himself, and with a sigh of relief he raised his eyes to offer a prayer of thanks. Then, seeing the little silver stars Gael had stuck on the ceiling, he went to a different place. . . .

That voice, he thought. It was *God's voice*. Doug knew it absolutely. And that voice, calling him out of the ditch, saved his daughter's life. He hated to think what might have happened if he hadn't found her when he did. Doug now knew that she needed help desperately, and he would make sure she got it.

The next few weeks were difficult, with tearful meetings with counselors and doctors. The results were wonderful, however. Gael managed to fight her depression and regain her will to live. She received lots of love from her family, and things got better with her friends, as things always do over time. She began to see that drastic moments don't always warrant drastic measures.

Gael was ultimately diagnosed as clinically depressed. Had she not received treatment, Doug is convinced that she would have found a way to end her life. But God had other plans, and today Gael is a bright, thriving eighteen-year-old, attending college and studying oceanography.

And Doug? He is deeply grateful. And aware, very aware, that God talks *directly* to human beings.

Most human beings believe that the opposite is true. We have been trained by our society—including, interestingly, many of our religions—to deny the possibility that God would speak directly to ordinary people. God *has* talked to human beings, we are told, but not in a very long time, and not to regular people. His communications are called *revelations*, and these were said to have been given only to very special people under very special circumstances.

If the "special" people who had these experiences (or those who heard about them) happened to write down the details, those writings were called Sacred Scriptures. The writings of any "regular person" sharing such experiences were called heresy.

Additionally, the closer someone's experience is to the present time, the more likely it is to be dismissed as delusional or hallucinatory. The further back in time such an experience recedes, the more likely it is to be honored.

George Bernard Shaw said, "All great truth begins as blasphemy."

Our job in this present culture of denial is *not* to deny the experience of our own soul, of our own mind, and of our own body, but to *declare it*. Loud and clear, for all to hear. That is not always easy.

For years, when the experience of my own soul, mind, or body (to say nothing of all three) ran counter to what I had been told was possible or true, I denied that experience. Many people do. Until they can't anymore. Until the evidence is so overwhelming, so profound, or so startling that denial is no longer possible.

Bill Colson would not deny his experience. Indeed, far from denying it, he stood up in front of a church filled with people at his father's memorial service and gave testimony to it. Bill Tucker would not deny his experience, either. Nor would David Daniel, Fred and Anne Ruth, Gerry Reid, or the other "regular people" whose stories appear in this book. They understand, they *know*, that God moves in their lives, that God interacts with human beings *directly*. That God even *speaks* to people. Do you think that Doug Furbush has any doubt about that?

I can tell you, he does not.

But the important thing to notice here is that his experience is not that unusual.

Robert Friedman is the publisher at Hampton Roads, the company that introduced the world to *Conversations with God*, and that published this book. When I first told Bob that I wanted to do a book called *Moments of Grace*, and explained to him what it was about, his immediate reaction was, "I've had one of those!"

"Really?" I asked.

"Absolutely. I know just what you're talking about."

"Well, tell me about it. What happened?"

"I was sixteen years old," Bob began, "and I had just learned to drive. This is in Portsmouth, Virginia."

"Uh-huh."

"Well, one day I was approaching a major four-lane high-way from a side road. At this particular stoplight there were hedges on both sides of the road. So the visibility was bad, real bad. But it didn't matter, because there was a stoplight, right?

"So when the light turns green, normally you just go. Well, the light turns green, and I start to put my foot on the accelerator, when all of a sudden a voice says '*Stop!*' Just like that. Just, *Stop!* I mean, there's no one else in the car, and I hear this voice, clear as a bell, and it just says, *Stop!*

"So I slam on the brake. It's purely an automatic reaction. I didn't even think about it. I just slammed on the brake. And this *guy* . . . this *car runs the light!* He's comin' from the left, I don't even see him, because of the hedge, before he gets right into the intersection, but he's doin' fifty miles an hour and he's flying.

"If I hadn't stopped, he'd have hit me right on the driver's side. I mean, this guy's really movin' and I'm a dead man out there. There's no doubt in my mind, I'da been dead.

"Now you tell me what that voice was. Was that an angel, a guardian angel? Was that my guide? Was that God? I don't know. I'm not even sure if there's a difference. I mean, it's all God manifesting, right? All I know is, *I—heard—that—voice.* Hey, it said only one word, but it saved my life."

"Whoa," I said. "And if it weren't for that Moment of Grace, there wouldn't have been this *Moments of Grace.*

The book, I mean. 'Cause you wouldn't have been here to publish it. You wouldn't even have been around to publish *Conversations with God*."

"I sure wouldn't."

"So I guess God had plans for you."

"I think He had plans for us both."

So there you have it. I think everybody has at least one personal story about Divine Intervention. And I'm not surprised. I told Bob that I wanted to do this book because I wanted to prove to the world that my experience in *Conversations with God* was not that unusual; that the only thing unusual about it was that I was willing to go public with it, to talk about it. And, I guess, that I continued the experience so long, and kept a record of it, and so I could write a book about it. But the experience itself, the experience of God communicating directly to us, that is very, very common.

If you're in Indianapolis, Indiana some day, ask Carolyn Leffler. Here's her experience, in her own words. . . .

6

God Sings, Too?

"Mom, don't worry about Dad," my five-year-old said, looking right into my eyes. "Everything will be okay."

I was startled, of course. Driving Eric to school, I had been lost in thought about my pending divorce proceeding. I had become resigned to the end of my marriage; what I was really worried about was its effect on Eric.

He and his father were close. I had tried to shield him from the harsh reality that his father would not be living with us anymore, but Eric was too smart and too sensitive to not know the truth.

After his dad actually left, Eric took to wearing his hooded sweatshirt backwards, covering his face whenever possible. No matter how I begged him, he continued to hide. But today he seemed able to come out of himself in order to offer me comfort.

"Thanks, honey. You're right. Everything is going to be fine."

I marveled again at Eric's ability to read my mind. He had been an intuitive child from the very beginning. He would pick up on my innermost thoughts when I least expected it, almost as if we communicated telepathically. We often played a game called "Think Me Home." When dinner was ready and it was time for Eric to come in from playing, I would direct my thoughts to Eric and mentally call him. Sure enough, Eric would soon come tramping in the door, saying almost matter-of-factly, "Okay. I'm here, Mommy."

Eric was very different from most children. Later, when he became old enough to go to school, I saw that the kids in his class didn't seem to understand him, and that because of this he often felt alienated. As a result, Eric had a very rich fantasy life. He often entered the world of his imagination without warning, becoming so totally immersed in it that he lost track of reality. In fact, his imagination would *become* his reality.

Once, when he was around eight, Eric became bored at school and sought refuge in his fantasy world. In his mind he became a tiger stalking his prey in the jungle. As he quietly and stealthily prowled through the dense, green foliage, he came upon a monkey foraging in the grass. Eric pounced at once and overcame his prey.

"Eric! What are you doing?" he heard his teacher yell. Eric came back to the present with a jolt. He was crouching on the floor of the schoolroom, biting the edge of his wooden desk! In humiliation, he apologized to the teacher. He told me later that he could not find the words to explain his behavior, and besides, by this time his teacher had given up on understanding him anyway, Eric thought.

I've always known that Eric's imaginary world, besides being a place of refuge and the source of his inability to "fit in" with other kids, was symptomatic of a special sensitivity to the aches and pains of every childhood. He was vulnerable to things that other children might easily shrug off.

It was when he was ten, at the beginning of recess one

day, that this trait showed itself in its most dangerous way. As Eric tells it, he had invited a classmate—Jason was his name, I think—to play some sort of game with him. Jason replied, "Nah. I'm gonna play football with the other guys. Wanna play with us?"

Eric recoiled. The last time he'd played football, he had been hit badly and came home with a black eye. "No way," he said.

"Well, I'm playing football," Jason came back. "You do what you want." There was a hurtful finality to it that really got to Eric. He may have moved immediately to the conclusion that since Jason wouldn't play with him, Jason did not like him—and from there to the idea that *no one* liked him.

If that's what he *was* thinking, I know it would have been unbearable for him. Eric found a jump rope that someone had discarded and, without a second thought, climbed onto a three-foot wall, tied one end of the rope around a fence and the other around his neck, and jumped.

Luckily, a teacher on playground duty chanced to look Eric's way a half-second before. Racing over to hold him, she yelled for another teacher to come over and loosen the rope around his neck.

Eric was not badly hurt, but he'd frightened everyone to death. I was called right away, and as I sat with Eric in the principal's office, tears streaked my face.

"Sweetie, why would you do that to yourself?" I asked him. "Don't you know that we can talk about whatever is hurting and work it out together? I love you. Your daddy loves you. God loves you."

"But nobody at *school* likes me, Mommy," Eric cried pitifully.

I put my arms around my son. How can I help him? I desperately wanted to know.

Discussing the incident with the school counselors, I

decided to give it as little attention as possible. Keeping the reaction low-key was thought to be the best way to handle it, by both the teachers and the counselors. I resolved to get Eric the help he needed to deal with the pain of his father's leaving the house.

Unfortunately, I didn't get the chance.

Only two days later, Eric attempted to hang himself again, this time on a hook in the coat closet. It was then that I made the difficult decision to admit Eric to a psychiatric hospital. I felt I had no other choice.

As we drove up the tree-lined avenue toward the facility, I cried inwardly, thinking, *I can't leave my baby in this strange place. He's only ten years old!* I wondered if Eric really understood that he would be living there, separated now not only from his father but also from me and all the things that he loved most . . . the home that was his haven, his refuge.

"Mom, don't worry. I'll be fine. You can visit me all the time."

Once again Eric had read my thoughts. *How can a child be so intuitive and so troubled at the same time?* I asked myself plaintively.

Leading Eric by the hand, I allowed the attendant to show us around the facility. The place was not unpleasant, but it was, after all, a hospital. We talked to doctors and nurses, unpacked his things, gave each other one last lingering hug, and said goodbye. I would not be able to see Eric for a whole week. I didn't think that I could bear being apart from my little boy. He needed me so much; he would be so alone. *Why did this have to happen?* I raged inwardly.

I was very distraught as I guided my car unconsciously through the city streets. All of my feelings had been held inside for days. Of course, I was trying to be strong for Eric, but now it was no longer necessary to stop the flow of tears, and I finally just let them flow.

In my mind I screamed, "Why is this *happening?* Where is someone to help *me . . .* to support *me!* I'm alone, *totally alone!*" I had to work hard to not collapse over the steering wheel.

As I parked the car and stumbled into my empty house, I knew I was in for a very lonely time. I fell onto my bed without removing my clothes, wrapping the chenille bedspread around me. Inside my cocoon, I sobbed out loud, wanting only to be held and comforted. Then I heard someone say, *You are not alone, Carolyn.*

I sprang upright in bed, looking around in surprise. The room was empty.

I am with you.

There it was *again.* That voice, coming from nowhere. This time, though, I felt neither startled nor uneasy. In fact, a wonderful sense of peace came over me. I suddenly felt that I knew who was speaking to me.

The voice softly embraced me and permeated my being. In relief, I lay back and fell into a deep, restful sleep.

The next morning, I awoke to the sun shining through my window. For the first time in days, hope filled my heart. I even caught myself humming as I dressed for work. I now felt—I now *knew*—that Eric was going to be okay. I also knew that I was going to pull through all of this just fine . . . with God's help.

Then, driving to work, doubt crept in.

Grow up, my parenting mind scolded. *You think things are going to be okay because all of a sudden you've got God on your side?*

I hated that. I hated when my down-to-earth, sometimes skeptical mind talked me out of feeling good—usually just when I was emotionally getting on top of things. *Don't!* I ordered myself. *Don't go there! Oh, God, help me. Help me to know that this is real, that you're here, that I didn't just imagine last night.*

Impulsively, looking for something to put me in a more positive mood, I reached over and turned on the radio. A tune immediately filled the car. "Now and forever," came the words, "I will always be with you."

I pulled over to the side of the road.

And cried.

Many years have passed since that day. And God kept His promise. He has always been with me. Eric has not only survived that challenge in his life, he is an incredible young man, who through his single-mindedness is pursuing his dream of being an entertainer. He is "CWG-inspired," as am I!

We made it.

Never doubt that God comes to us in answer to our call. Yet always be aware that the Forms of God are multitudinous. And endless.

It is as I said. God is shameless. The plotline of the next movie you see. The message on a giant billboard around the corner. A comment overhead from the next table at a restaurant. "All these devices are Mine," God says in *Conversations with God*. She will apparently stop at nothing to get us to see what we next need to see, to know what we next need to know.

I will never forget the story an elderly lady—Gladys, I think her name was—told me in a letter some years ago. She'd been reading my book and was having some troubles in her life, and so she was having difficulty believing what she was seeing in *CWG*.

"Okay, God," she barked out loud one day, wandering around her small apartment. "If you're real like Neale says you are, show yourself to me. Come on. Give me a sign. *Any* sign. I don't care. Just give me some kind of sign that you're real, that you're alive, that you're *here right now*."

Nothing happened.

She sat on the stool at her kitchen counter, sipping coffee.
Nothing happened.

She moved to her overstuffed rocker, closing her eyes
and waiting.

Nothing.

"Yeah," she muttered finally. "That's what I thought."

She got up in disgust and turned on the TV. Then she
went pale. Her legs turned to rubber. She backed herself
into the rocker, her face frozen in disbelief. Two words, big
as life, filled the television screen:

OH, GOD

The John Denver–George Burns movie had just begun,
the movie's title burning into view precisely as Gladys hit
the ON button. You can't even imagine what went through
her mind.

She chuckled about it later, and her letter was written in
that lighthearted spirit. But she never again doubted the
existence—or the presence—of God.

And so you see, God reveals Himself to us in many
forms. Not all of them are "God-like." Heavenly messages
do not always come to us in heavenly packages or through
heavenly experiences, the way we would expect them to.
They can be delivered in hot rock songs. Or twenty-year-old
movie titles. Or widely popular, if improbable, books.

Seldom are God's messages accompanied by heavenly
harps, or delivered to us by angels.

Seldom.

But I wouldn't say never. . . .

7

A Messenger from Heaven?

Denise Moreland looked over at the new mother in the hospital bed next to hers. The young woman wore a radiant smile as she nursed her newborn girl.

Why can't I be holding my own healthy baby? Denise asked God in the privacy of her mind. *Why does this woman have her child in her arms while mine lies in the nursery, hanging between life and death?*

It was the winter of 1976, the year of America's bicentennial. While many people were celebrating life, liberty, and the pursuit of happiness, Denise was pursuing something even more basic—a reason to live. After two miscarriages before the age of eighteen, she had finally managed to carry this baby to full term. But something had gone terribly wrong. Late in her pregnancy, Denise's O-negative blood had begun attacking her unborn baby's O-positive, and it had been necessary to deliver him by emergency C-section last night. Little Adam was now fighting for his life, and the doctors hadn't given Denise a great deal of hope that he would make it.

"He's so tiny, and so beautiful." Denise felt so alone as she gazed at Adam lying in the cold, plastic crib with tubes running in and out of him. She longed to hold him and warm him, and assure him of her love. He was only six-and-one-half pounds. Denise didn't see how anything so small and helpless could fight hard enough to live.

But fight he did. As Adam struggled for the next few days, Denise also found herself fighting—fighting not to hate the woman one bed over who cooed and lovingly nursed her baby every few hours. More than that, she fought to not hate the God who appeared to have abandoned her.

The bleak scene outside the hospital window didn't help matters; the city was blanketed with snow and ice. The hospital was literally cut off from the outside world of visitors coming and going. Denise felt alone and imprisoned in a reality she simply could not grasp—that her son might die.

As she lay in bed the third night, trying not to think about the possibility of actually going home without her baby, Denise filled with rage.

How can you do this to me, God? she screamed inwardly. *How could you give me this child, this long-awaited family—especially after the horrible childhood I suffered through—only to take him away from me?* Denise thought her heart would break.

Unable to cope with the fierce battle of emotions raging within her, Denise picked up a pen to write a friend with whom she'd enjoyed a correspondence for years. Long ago Denise had become accustomed to pouring out her emotions on paper to this friend, and it seemed that now she needed to vent more than ever before.

As the pen moved swiftly across the paper, all the mental anguish and deep sense of injustice poured out of her and was given voice. Denise hardly had a conscious thought as she scribbled on the paper. The writing continued to flow as she filled page after page. The terrible pain in her heart finally began to ease. Then, suddenly, even as she wrote, she realized that she was no longer pouring out her heart to her friend. She was talking to God. Denise stopped to read the words that had just come from her.

"This child is a true blessing to me, and I am so in love with him. He is a gift from God—conceived by me—but God's son. While I do not understand why He would take my baby from me, I realize there is nothing I can do about it. If the Father wants to take Adam home, so be it. If God gave him to me, God can take him back. I have to believe there is a reason, a divine plan. So, Master Creator, do what is in keeping with the higher good. Not my will, but Thine."

It was the first time in Denise's life that she felt she had actually communicated with God. Oh, she'd talked to God before, heaven knows. Most recently in her angry outbursts. Yet she had never felt that she was actually *communicating* with anybody. But now . . . now she felt for the first time in her life that she'd actually spoken to God. And there was more. She also felt that God had *heard* her, had agreed with her, had even spoken some thoughts *through* her, *to* her. He was bringing her understanding, she saw now. Where else would she have come up with those words in her letter? They had certainly not been *her* thoughts.

Until now.

Feeling strangely calm, she put the pages on the bedside table, turned out the light, and slept soundly for the first time in three days.

"Good morning, Denise." The nurse touched her gently on the shoulder. "I came to tell you that we'll be drawing Adam's blood today to determine if he needs a transfusion."

Even half asleep, Denise understood the implications of this news. If Adam were to require a transfusion, all kinds of complications could arise. The new blood could save his life, or end it.

Smoothing Denise's pillow, the nurse whispered gently, "Keep the faith, honey." With a soft smile, she slipped out of the room.

Denise thought of how easy it must be to say those words, and how difficult it is to actually be faithful in times like these. As she stared out the window, she searched for the lifeless winter sun. It hardly seemed like morning. Everything was so quiet. Odd, how snow muffles sound so completely, she mused. In the silence and grayness, Denise imagined her son in her arms, then saw him being lifted into God's hands. Once again she prayed, "Thy will be done."

Denise suddenly felt oddly flushed and weak. Then a sharp pain stabbed her groin, hurting so much that involuntarily she folded inward. The room grew darker, and Denise watched with a strange detachment as the scene before her receded . . . and then disappeared altogether. She lost consciousness.

"You can go home if you choose," Denise heard someone saying. She opened her eyes to find a beautiful woman standing beside her bed. What had happened to her, and who was this person? Her head spinning, Denise struggled to see more clearly. It did not appear as if the visitor was actually talking; instead, her melodic voice seemed to be coming from somewhere inside Denise's head.

The lady looked deep into Denise's eyes. "The Father stands ready to receive you, if that is what you desire. But I must tell you, your work here is not finished; your purpose is not yet fulfilled. Your little son will live. There is much for you yet to experience and learn on this path."

She was dressed in an exquisite gown of flowing black chiffon. Her dark hair fell about her shoulders. Denise had thought an angel would be wearing white, but this seemed somehow appropriate, and the woman was so beautiful. Her eyes were filled with compassion and love—so much love that Denise could hardly comprehend it.

"God honors your choice in all things," she seemed to be saying. "You have called unto yourself some difficult lessons, but these lessons prepare you for your service to others, should you choose to remain. Time and time again you will be called upon to remember your faith."

Denise knew without a doubt that she was being presented with an opportunity—to continue to live in this world, or to move beyond, into a new adventure. Life was precious, she knew that. But it was also very difficult. Hadn't her years up to this point been a constant battle with pain and fear?

Even now she was struggling with the awful reality that her baby could die and that she could remain childless for the rest of her life. She could choose, right now, to just leave. To go. This loving presence was offering to take her home, back to the Father's arms, where there would be peace.

But Denise knew she wanted to stay. Her baby was going to live! And in time, she herself would become healthy and happy again, with a family to care for and a life to live. Turning her face to her special angel, Denise saw that she was smiling, already knowing what Denise's decision was.

"I am with you always," the angel said. Then, she was gone.

Denise blinked . . . and saw the nurse standing over her, holding Adam in her arms. With incredible joy, she reached out for her baby boy.

Something wonderful happened to Denise Moreland when she began writing that letter to a friend. She let go of her anger and released her resistance to what was occurring. This was an important turning point in her experience.

Friendship with God says:

> Then, accept it, and resist not evil. For what you resist, persists. Only what you accept can you change.

Now, envelop it with love. Whatever you are experiencing, you can literally love any undesired experience away. In a sense, you can "love it to death."

Finally, be joyful, for the exact and perfect outcome is at hand. Nothing can take your joy away from you, for joy is Who You Are. So, in the face of every problem, do a joyful thing.

Denise's experience is also a wonderful illustration of how God's wisdom can come right through us, even at the most unexpected times. Perhaps especially so.

Denise got out a sheet of paper and began writing a letter to a friend. Before she knew it, she was writing a letter to God. And that letter to God was actually comforting *her*. The wisdom she was expressing was meant for her, and it was brought *to* her, *through* her.

Over and over again *Conversations with God* tells us to listen to our internal voice, to go within, to seek the wisdom that resides in our soul. The soul, *CWG* says, is the closest part of God to us.

Now Denise got in touch with that part of herself "by accident." (Of course, there are no accidents. Nothing happens in life by chance. But you know what I mean.) She began writing to one person and ended up writing to *someone else altogether*.

Imagine what might have happened had she started *out* writing a letter to God! I mean, *deliberately and everything* . . .

Whoa. You don't suppose she'd wind up with a book, do you?

Denise's experience is also a wonderful illustration of how wrong we can be if we really believe that God's messages are seldom delivered to us by angels. Actually, they are always delivered to us by angels.

In one form or another.

But wait a minute. Could this be true? Are there such things as angels? Really?

Yes.

The answer is, yes.

They watch over us. They take care of us. And they lead us Home when our stay here is over. They hover over us and they walk with us and they stand by our side night and day, through good times and bad, in sickness and in health, until death do us meet.

Remember what Denise's angel told her? "I am with you always." She wasn't lying. Angels don't lie. Angels bless us and protect us and guide us to our highest good.

They can come to us as dreams, during meditations as visions, and even when we are wide awake, as apparitions. But now, here may be the surprising part. I believe that angels also come to us as "real-life people," walking around just like you and me, showing up in our lives and doing or saying incredible things.

Maybe that's fanciful thinking, but I think the world could do with some fanciful thinking. And then, there's another way to look at it. God says in *CWG*, "I have sent you nothing but angels."

This means that *everybody* is an angel! They have all come from God and have entered your life on a mission. Perhaps that "mission" is known only at the soul level, but it *is known* at that level, and to both of you.

Surprised?

Consider this. At a very deep level, we may very well know why we are entering each other's lives. Because this is so, we send off, we "emit" from that same deep level, vibes—I mean, actual *vibrations*—that indicate our purpose. This is why, when you meet someone, you sometimes feel that "something is up," something's going to go on with that person.

Let me tell you about when I first met Nancy, who is now my wife. The moment she walked up to me, I knew something was up. I just knew.

Ever have that feeling?

Yes?

Ah, well . . . do you think this is something that you're making up?

Wrong.

Nancy barely got within six feet of me when a feeling came over me. It was not a feeling of sunshine on my shoulders and bells ringing in my ears and my heart melting. I didn't see stars, and fireworks did not go off. But the feeling was just as impactful in its own way. I felt as if my whole body had been put on heightened alert. That's the only way I can describe it. It was kind of like, *hey, wake up.*

And then, I actually heard words. In my mind I heard, very directly and very pointedly: *This person is going to be very important to you.*

I had no idea what that was about. I had no idea what was going on. But I can tell you that I looked at that very closely. I paid attention to that moment.

I consider that to have been a Moment of Grace.

Months later, when I had to make a major decision about commitment, about what role I wanted to play in Nancy's life and what role I wanted her to play in mine, I remembered that message. And this may sound a little "airy-fairy," a little "way out," but I made my decision based on that moment. And I have never, not for one minute, regretted it.

So people come into your life with a mission. No one shows up by chance. Not even the passerby on the street. Not even the waitress at the restaurant (who keeps changing every week).

No one shows up by chance.

When we're alert, when we're awake, we start to look at who's coming into our life right now and we ask, what is the opportunity here? What is going on right now? What is the gift I have a chance to receive? What is the gift I have a chance to give?

Maybe coming into your life is an angel in a dream, as with Denise, helping her to clearly see what her choices are right now. Don't dismiss that as fantasy or "just my imagination." What would you think if it were *real*?

Maybe it's an angel on a playground—a teacher who "just happens" to look Eric's way as he prepares to jump from a wall with a noose around his neck. Don't dismiss that as coincidence, or "just plain luck." What would you think if it were *by design*?

Maybe it's Eric himself, playing out his role perfectly so that all those whose lives he will touch may play out theirs. Don't dismiss that as off-the-wall, or "just a wild theory." What would you think if it were *true*?

Maybe it's you.

Had you ever thought of that?

Maybe you're the angel in someone else's life today. Don't dismiss that as unbelievable or "just wishful thinking." What would you think if it were *exactly what's so*?

In fact, it is.

The only question now is whether you believe it.

Now some people hear this kind of thing and "get" it right away. Others . . . well, others are a little stubborn, and it takes them a while.

Take Gerry Reid, for instance. . . .

8

A Fortunate Misfortune

Gerry Reid tells the story about a man who had a wonderful mule that he loved dearly, although it wouldn't do a thing it was ordered to do. The owner took the mule to a renowned animal trainer and asked if it was possible to teach the thing to obey. The trainer said, "Sure, leave him with me for a few days and when you come back, he'll be a new mule."

As the owner was leaving, he looked back to say goodbye and saw the trainer hitting the mule over the head with a two-by-four. "I asked you to train him, not to kill him!" the owner said angrily. To which the trainer replied, "Sometimes you just have to get their attention."

A lot of folks who knew Fred Ruth during those last weeks of difficulty with his heart may have been tempted to call him a mule. It took a bolt of lightning in his living room to get his attention. And Gerry Reid of Whitby, Ontario, will tell you that he felt just like that mule. God had gotten his attention all right. It had taken a good fifty years, give or take a few, but, like Fred Ruth, he got his wake-up call.

All his life, Gerry had been a pretty happy guy, enjoying the fruits of his labors, living day to day and enjoying it. He had never had much occasion to think about his soul, or the thing called Deity. When he thought about this at all, it was mostly to doubt God's existence. He was simply too busy with his life to pay attention to such things.

A few years back, when Gerry was earning his living as a printer, he had the foresight to realize that computers were going to radically change his industry, so he set out to train himself in the latest computer desktop technology. That proved to be fortuitous, because Gerry was eventually laid off from his job of many years.

When he lost his job, he looked for schools that offered advanced desktop-publishing training so that he could reestablish himself in his chosen profession. But rather than discover classes for which he could sign up as a student, Gerry found that he was being offered the opportunity to be an instructor.

It seemed that what he had taught himself was more than most people had learned. And thus it came to pass that in a few short weeks Gerry went from being a printer to being a computer trainer. He found that computers were easy to teach because the process was so linear; each step was followed by another logical step. Further, teaching seemed to come naturally to him. He enjoyed the college atmosphere; the students were friendly and eager to learn.

One day as he was having coffee in the student lounge, Gerry noticed one of the students making a little bit of a commotion at a nearby table. He ambled over, trying to act as casual as possible.

"So, Dan, what's up with you today?" he asked.

Most people at the college knew that Dan had sustained a brain injury after a New Year's Eve accident the previous year. A car had hit him as he was crossing a busy street, and ever since then, he had become quite volatile. Dan was now taking business courses as a form of therapy, and teachers and students were used to his occasional outbursts in the classroom. Rage is a common symptom of brain injury.

"The teachers don't like me and I don't like the teachers," Dan was shouting in the student lounge. "I can't learn anything! I'm gonna quit!"

It must be very difficult for him, thought Gerry. Then he had an idea.

"Well," he said to Dan, "since you've paid your tuition already, why don't you just change over to my class? You might like computers."

That conversation proved to be a turning point for both Dan and Gerry. To everyone's great surprise, Dan excelled in the class. As it turned out, the linear, step-by-step learning process that Gerry employed was a method that a damaged brain could understand more easily, allowing it to develop effectiveness with a skill at an accelerated pace.

Dan flourished, and soon his therapist came in to talk with Gerry, wanting to find out what he had done to contribute to Dan's mental and emotional improvement. Dan was suddenly far less angry and much more in control of his responses to difficult situations. It seemed that Gerry had found another talent—implementing healing therapy for the brain-injured.

It was then that the two-by-four hit him.

While he was riding along on his motorcycle one day, a tire blew. The bike flipped over and landed squarely on Gerry's head. He lay in the road, unconscious and bleeding, his body terribly broken. The man driving the car behind Gerry came to his immediate rescue. The man, as it turned out, was a vacationing emergency medical technician.

He stayed with Gerry, attending to him until an ambulance arrived. The doctors later told Gerry that the paramedic had saved his life with his immediate and knowledgeable medical care. Of course, Gerry had no memory of any of this happening. He was in a coma for many days and awoke with very limited recall.

His brain had been damaged.

This is Gerry's memory:

While lying unconscious in the hospital bed, bandaged from head to toe, he opened his eyes to find himself standing before the entrance to a triangular-shaped tunnel. It was glowing green, undulating and alive. Gerry had felt a terrific yearning to step into the tunnel, but just as he was about to he saw someone standing over to one side.

"You may not enter, Gerry," the person seemed to say, but without really using words. "It is not yet time. But you may touch."

Gerry stared at the entity in amazement. It was . . . what? Not a man or a woman . . . maybe it was an angel. . . .

Angels, angels . . . Gerry searched his mind. *What do I know about angels? Nothing other than that they're mostly named "Michael."* "Are you Michael?" Gerry directed the question to the being before him.

There was no response at first, but Gerry got the distinct feeling that the Being was somehow amused. "If you would like to call me that, you may," the angel then seemed to say.

Gerry reached out and felt the green wall of the tunnel. It was soft and pliable, and some of it came off easily onto his hand. Immediately he had the strange thought that he should rub this stuff on his arm—the arm that was so horribly injured in the accident. As he applied the green material to his damaged limb, *the pain stopped*. Gerry took a deep breath.

Relief.

"Thank you," he began, but the angel had disappeared, along with the tunnel. All Gerry could see now was a triangle hanging above him . . . and then, the hospital bed. The triangle appeared to be some kind of apparatus hanging from the ceiling. The hospital room was slowly beginning to come into focus. Gerry saw that he was covered in bandages. He couldn't move, but his arm no longer hurt. And he was definitely alive!

Finally released from the hospital after weeks of arduous recovery, and with his own brain injury, Gerry found that he had little stamina for the long hours required to be a teacher. He began to volunteer for a few hours a day at the local chapter of the Brain Injury Association. His computer expertise was useful to the staff, and when one of the directors learned that teaching computer software was becoming an accepted form of therapy for their constituency, she approached Gerry about developing a business on his own.

"We are not in a position to provide this type of service, but we can certainly refer people to you if they are interested," she offered. Was this conversation yet another manifestation of Divine Intervention? All Gerry knows is that he is now a successful, happy, and healthy owner of a business that provides computer-skills therapy to persons with brain injuries—and that it is beautiful to watch people, many of whom have come to believe that they cannot learn anything new, grow and develop.

Meanwhile, Gerry says his personal angel—Michael, or so Gerry continues to call him—visits him often. The visits usually occur when Gerry is in need of emotional assistance, but there is never any way of knowing when he will appear. There aren't any halos or wings, and if Gerry tries to tightly focus, or becomes too inquisitive, Michael slips away. But he is a continuing, helpful, loving presence in Gerry's life. Just as Gerry has tried to be in the lives of all those he is hoping to help.

<hr/>

You see? Gerry has decided to be a loving, helpful angel in the lives of others. He "gets" it! He is the angel in someone else's life today! And he lives out that role in every way he knows how.

Can you imagine what kind of world this would be if we all did that?

But it's not always easy, and I think we should acknowledge that. We are, after all, mired deeply within our illusions on this planet. *Communion with God* describes this experience in very specific terms, outlining what it calls The Ten Illusions of Humans (Need, Failure, Separation, Insufficiency, Requirement, Judgment, Condemnation, Conditionality, Superiority, Ignorance).

Because we live so completely and so convincingly within our illusions, we very, very seldom see things as they really are. For instance, we see what we call "bad" as "bad" and what we call "good" as "good," and we do not see how the two can be interchanged, or, even more unbelievable to us, the same thing at once.

Yet it is a great truth that sometimes what we have called the biggest tragedy of our lives turns out to be the greatest gift we have ever received. In fact—and this is hard to believe, I know, so hold tight here—that is *always the case*.

Remember when I said that God told me, "I have sent you nothing but angels"? Well, He also told me, "I have given you nothing but miracles."

What is this? Is God saying that *everything* is a miracle? Yes.

Now when you consider that life itself is a miracle—that the fact that life as we know it even evolved on this planet in the way that it did is utterly miraculous—it becomes easier to understand and accept that everything *within* life is a miracle. But I don't think God meant Her statement to be so sweeping, and thus so meaningless. I think that God meant that everything, *specifically*, that we have been given is a miracle.

If that is true, how are we to experience this? How are we to come to such a conclusion?

Conversations with God gives us three golden words to remember when facing a tragedy or difficult circumstances.

See the Perfection.

This may not always be easy, but when it is done it can turn moments of despair into Moments of Grace.

Whenever I talk about this concept in my lectures or retreats, I am always inspired to use as an example the story of Christopher Reeve.

Mr. Reeve, as most of you know, is the dashing and wonderful actor who stopped our hearts in *Somewhere in Time* and thrilled our imaginations in *Superman* and entertained us so fabulously in many other vehicles. His film career seemed to be cruelly cut short by a horseback-riding accident in which he wound up being paralyzed from the neck down.

Now at first glance this could look like a terrible tragedy. And certainly, it has not been easy for Mr. Reeve. No one would suggest that. But stay with me here. I want us to look at something.

Since his accident, Christopher Reeve has become the most powerful, the most eloquent, and by far the most influential spokesperson in the world for people who are physically challenged. And that is not a small thing, because people who are physically challenged have *needed* an eloquent and powerful voice.

Christopher Reeve has raised millions of dollars in contributions for research programs designed to produce all manner of beneficial outcomes for persons who are paralyzed—including the possibility of condition reversals in some cases.

But Mr. Reeve has done more than raise the hopes of the physically challenged for a better quality of life tomorrow. He has caused thousands of them to experience a better quality of life today, by becoming an inspiring example of what can be done with one's life *regardless of one's physical condition.*

Not only has he traveled extensively for fund- and consciousness-raising activities, but he has also returned to his career in the dramatic arts, as both an actor and a director, with magnificent results.

How has he done this? What is his secret?

Well, I have never spoken to Christopher Reeve, but I am willing to wager anything that it has to do with his *point of view* about things. Somewhere along the line after his accident, I believe that Mr. Reeve made a decision, first of all, that he wanted to live. Second, that he wanted to live fruitfully, engagingly, actively, and purposefully. And third, that it was *possible for him to do so,* and that nothing could stop him if he really tried.

Here is something that I have been told in my conversations with God that has appeared in virtually all of my books: Perception is everything.

Now here is something that I have been told that has *never* made it into any of my books. (It came to me "between" books, and I never found a way to "work it in"!): Perception is the third step in the Process of Ceiving.

The Process of Ceiving? Yes, that's what I said. Now this is something that God gave me in a conversation one night.

He said,

Neale, all of life is a Process of Ceiving.

Ceiving? I repeated. What is Ceiving?

And She replied,

It is a word we are going to make up, out of the language that you speak, so that you may better understand a principle that is so extraordinary, there is no word in your language with which to describe it.

So we're going to create one.

Yes. Is that okay?

Hey, you're the boss.

Well, not actually. You are. But I can live with your characterization of Me for the moment. Now, do you remember when I told you long ago that words are the least reliable form of communication?

Yes.

Well, this is a perfect example. Your language has no word to precisely describe something that goes on in your life every day. So we're going to take a portion of some of your words, and use that. We're going to call this experience the Process of Ceiving.

And, I assume, you're going to explain it to me.

I am indeed. "Ceiving" is the process by which you create your personal reality. It goes like this. First, you have an idea. This is an act of pure creation. You create something in your mind. You, quite literally, conceive it. Then, you look at what you have created and you make a judgment about it. You have an opinion about what you have conceived. You take a point of view about what you originally conceived. You, quite literally, perceive it.

Now, it is how you look at what has been created, not what was originally created, that becomes your experience. You quite literally receive it.

What you conceive you perceive, and what you perceive you receive.

The process is:

Conception.

Perception.

Reception.

If you stay close to your original idea, what you re-Ceive will be very close to what you con-Ceive. This is where Masters live, and their highest ideas become their grandest reality. Yet you often—too often—see things differently than you first saw them (just as you see yourself differently than you first saw you), because you imagine your first idea too good to be true. You thus move away from your original idea. You can then be fooled about what is true. That is, you can be, quite literally, de-Ceived.

I was, as you can imagine, flabbergasted when I was given this information. Nothing I had ever heard came even close to describing the mental process of creation as clearly as this.

I understand now that when we "see the perfection" in all things, what we are simply doing is staying close to our soul's original idea, which had no imperfection in it. Then the glory and the wonder of Original Intention can be made manifest in our lives. We are no longer de-Ceived. We see Moments of Grace where we would never have seen them before.

When was Fred Ruth's Moment of Grace? Was it when he, quite literally, "saw the light"? Of course. Everyone recognizes that as a Moment of Grace. Everyone sees that as a miracle. But Fred had another Moment of Grace that might not be immediately apparent. It was when he had his first cardiac episode. He may have experienced it differently at the time. He might have called it a moment of misfortune. But that would have been because he did not see the perfection, for he could not then see the path he has now taken, nor know what was required in order to take it.

All of us have many Moments of Grace, whether we know it or not. It is not as if we are allocated one per lifetime.

Gerry Reid's Moments of Grace? One was when he got laid off from the job he'd held for many years. Another was when he met Dan, the brain-damaged student, at the college. A third was when the tire blew out on his motorcycle. And a fourth was most definitely when he "saw" the entity he calls Michael.

When we look back on them, we can often see how these special moments have created a chain link, a connected pipeline, an extraordinary glide path from where we were to where we wanted to be. As we look to our future, we can see the same pipeline, the same glide path, but only if we know that it is there.

Sometimes it is not very obvious. . . .

9

Divine Designs

Troy Butterworth remembers when, as a young boy, he lay beside his mother, holding her in his arms while she sobbed.

"If only you could just leave him, Mom," he said, trying desperately to convince her once again to escape her husband's abuse. There had been many nights just like this when Troy had begged her to get away from his father. He shuddered as he remembered the coldness in his father's voice earlier that night.

"You try to divorce me, bitch, and I'll slit your throat," he had threatened.

Neither one of them doubted his words.

Troy wiped his mother's tears. "If I try to leave him, what will happen to you and your brothers and sisters? I can't leave you alone with him, Troy. I have to stay," she sobbed.

Lately the abuse had gotten worse. Not only was his mother routinely beaten, but the sick sexual games his drunken father liked to play with Troy and his brothers had become almost unbearable. These had started years before, when he was barely seven.

These days, when his dad was drinking heavily, Troy would hide in the closet. He'd longingly touch the guns stored back behind the hanging coats with morbid fantasies of pulling the trigger and blowing his father into little pieces. Sometimes he'd even search around in the dark for the bullets, as if he were really going to act out these fantasies.

Things were no better away from home. At school, where he was in the sixth grade, he was called "Gay Troy." It was because he didn't have the interests of the other boys. He didn't look or act like them, either. At recess he would try to hide from the gang that relentlessly chased him, throwing rocks and taunting him. They eventually ran him down and beat him up. Because he was always so afraid, he couldn't concentrate, so his grades were poor.

In addition to this physical torture, Troy was constantly haunted by the memories of being raped by his neighbor's boyfriend three years earlier. By then his life had been so full of abuse that he hardly recognized the incident as abnormal.

Remarkably, in spite of everything, Troy had a deep and close relationship with God. It often seemed that God was the only one who loved him. All through the pain of his childhood, Troy held fast to the one thought that God would not abandon him. It gave him comfort when there was no comfort to be found anywhere else. Still, even knowing that God loved him, he was wracked with guilt, because he knew—he now found himself admitting—that he *was* gay.

It wasn't really clear to Troy how God could love someone who was so sinful, so as he got older he began to question God's love.

One day his remorse became too painful to bear alone, and Troy decided to unburden himself. He sought the counsel of the preacher of the Baptist Church where he had gone for refuge so many times before. Everyone told him what the Bible said about homosexuality. God would forgive anything, they said, any sin—except that one. "But maybe they're wrong," Troy hoped. "Maybe God could love me just as I am." He so wanted that to be true.

"If you remain in God's grace," said the pastor, as the sunlight shone through the windows of his office and lit his desk, "you will go to heaven." Troy beamed, his hopes coming alive. The others had been wrong after all. "But if you cannot overcome your homosexuality," the pastor continued, "you will be beyond the grace of God."

Troy's heart plummeted. God, who had been his only friend, the one comfort in his life when there was no other, had turned His back. The preacher seemed uncomfortable hearing Troy's confession, and embarrassed to talk about it any further. What he couldn't seem to say outright, but what Troy understood completely, was that if you are gay, you are condemned to hell.

Now Troy had something else to be afraid of. First his father's abuse, then the beatings from his classmates, and now, being sent straight to hell.

Nothing would have made Troy happier than to wake up one morning and discover himself to be straight. "Please, God," he prayed every day, "*Please*. Make me straight."

But God didn't make Troy straight. As he grew older and his sexual energies bloomed, Troy tried, but he couldn't curb his desire to be with men. Convinced that God no longer loved him anyway, Troy eventually stopped even trying not to be gay. Or, for that matter, discreet. He became rebellious. He took an "If I'm damned anyway, what the hell" attitude. He brazenly started looking for sex in public places.

He had sex with anyone and everyone who was willing—in parks, in public rest rooms, in sex clubs where one could go and, for a small sum of money, have sex any time of the day or night. He was on a binge. He couldn't stop, no matter how he tried or how much he wanted things to be different.

God was gone, his mother was now in a mental institution,

and life was meaningless. Abuse was so much a part of Troy's existence that in its absence he could only abuse himself. So he fled to New York where he could find more sexual partners and try to fill the void that losing God had left in his heart.

On Troy's twenty-third birthday, Christmas Day, there had been no cards, no phone calls from his family, no contact from any human being. It was gray and rainy. The dreary streets were empty. Troy didn't have one friend in New York. He sat in his dingy, bleak apartment, listening to the traffic below, feeling that his life had reached its lowest point. He was cold and lonely.

I don't have to be alone, damn it, he ruminated. He knew there was a sex club a few blocks away that he hadn't checked out yet. *To hell with it. I'm going over there.* Troy defiantly pulled on his coat and left his apartment, heading for the only comfort he knew. *At least I'll be able to have some human contact*, he sighed as he braved the windy street.

"There's no one here but me," said the manager. He looked rather youthful and clean-cut for a sex-club operator.

"You'll do fine," said Troy, sauntering over to the couch.

"No, man. I don't do the customers. I just run the joint. It's Christmas. Nobody's here."

"Just let me make love to you. Please." Troy needed desperately to feel a human's touch. He wanted sex.

"I told you, man. I don't have sex with the customers. This is just a job. I do this so I can pay for my tuition. I'm not into doing the customers."

Troy was frantic; he had to have sex, he just had to. But the man continued to talk—something about going to school and having a boyfriend. Troy couldn't listen. All he could do was feel his neediness, his desperation.

Then, without warning, the room became dim and Troy started to feel dizzy and disoriented. Something very strange happened. Troy found himself looking at the room from the vantage point of somewhere else. He was no longer in his body; he was across the room observing himself, sitting on the torn, dirty, orange-and-brown couch. The young manager was standing over him, talking away. "What's happening?" Troy asked with alarm. "What's going on?"

Then, as quickly as he had left his body, he returned to it. His head slowly cleared as he slumped on the couch in disgust. He had never felt so sickened and repelled in his life. Not in all those years of being violated by his father and assaulted by classmates, or even when he had been brutally raped, had he felt such self-loathing. Not even when he thought of all those men he never even knew who responded to his advances. Now here he was, begging for sex. Acting crude. Coming on. Troy wanted to die.

It was in that moment that he decided to kill himself. But, he decided, before he died he'd have as much sex as he possibly could. In blind shame and disgust, he left the sex club and went on the binge to end all binges, spending the next three days roaming the streets, searching out parks and public rest rooms, and engaging in sex with any and every willing man he could find—three days of desperation, shame, fear, and total surrender to his addiction—an addiction that would not let him go, but which would not give him any peace.

On the third day, exhausted and totally devoid of any sense of himself whatsoever, he fled to the street to find yet another sex partner, remembering his resolve to soon end his life.

Walking fast and feeling feverish even in the rainy cold, he remembered from some conversation somewhere that in order to commit suicide with over-the-counter sleeping pills you needed to chase them with alcohol. He stopped into a liquor store and bought a bottle of Kahlua. Leaving the store, his eye caught the sign on the building across the street.

GAY AND LESBIAN CENTER.
ACTIVITIES 365 DAYS A YEAR. WELCOME.

Though he couldn't explain it and didn't understand it, Troy suddenly felt an overwhelming desire to go inside—as if he were being *urged* to do so. He stuffed the bottle into his backpack and crossed the street.

The lady at the reception desk told him simply, "The only meeting going on today is the Sexual Compulsives Anonymous meeting." Troy turned to leave, but something stopped him. "Where is the meeting?" he asked timidly.

"Down the hall, first door on the right."

Following her directions, he took a seat in the back of a small room. His palms were sweating. He felt nervous. The weight of the Kahlua in his backpack reminded him of his resolve, but right now he just wanted to talk to someone, anyone, before he went back to his apartment to face the finality of his decision.

"My name is Jane, and I am a sexual addict," a young woman standing at the front of the room was saying. "I've come here today because, at holiday times especially, I tend to act out." She appeared frightened.

Over the course of the evening, as he listened to one person's story after another, Troy would discover what he already knew but hadn't given voice to. He, too, was an addict. It wasn't an easy thing to admit. Troy knew by evening's end that he could no longer live his life in constant dread and disgust. It was recover or die. He saw it clearly now.

He had seen the desperation on the face of the Troy who sat on that filthy couch, begging for love; he had felt the cold loneliness of his empty apartment on a Christmas birthday; he held the memory of a painful childhood in which his mother's hopelessness mirrored his own despair. Now a thought occurred to him. *Maybe I can recover; perhaps there is hope.* Looking around the room, Troy said to himself,

These people are alive. They're troubled just like me, but at least they're doing something to try to heal their pain. He felt a tiny spark of life somewhere deep in his chest.

Troy went back to his apartment. He did not drink the Kahlua. Nor did he try to kill himself. Instead, he sat and reflected on all he had been through the previous three days, trying to sort things out.

The next morning, out of habit more than desire, he arose, dressed himself, and took the train to work. He spotted what appeared to be an empty space and headed toward it, but instead of an available seat, he found a homeless man lying across two places, sound asleep. Troy's first reaction was disgust and anger. He just wanted to sit and rest. Why was this person taking up two spaces?

He looked around and couldn't see another seat open. *Why, with everything else that's going on, do I have to deal with this?* Troy asked himself, utterly despondent. *Why is everything so difficult?*

God loves this person, too came a thought. It was like a bolt of lightning in his head. *You're the fortunate one.*

Troy almost looked around to see who had spoken, but he knew that the voice had come from his own heart. Yes, he was lonely and despondent, and he was disgusted with this life, but at least he'd had a meal that day, and tonight he would sleep in a clean bed in a place he could call his own. Even more importantly, God had given him the gift of hope. He had shown Troy his despair and led him directly to a 12-Step program.

Then Troy heard another thought. *God loves you, too.*

A special kind of warmth spread through his being, and then came an amazing revelation. *They're wrong. All those people who have told me over and over that I could never be truly loved by God, that I am condemned because of who and what I am, are wrong. Absolutely and unequivocally wrong.*

Examples of God's grace began to fill Troy's mind—occurrences which demonstrated God's presence in his life. Not only finding Sexual Compulsives Anonymous at a time when he had decided to commit suicide. There was more. Much more. Despite the threat of AIDS, he was still healthy. He'd never gotten in trouble with the law, even with all his public sexual activity. And, perhaps most important of all, he'd survived his childhood with his humanity intact.

According to every religious authority he'd ever heard, God wasn't supposed to love him enough to care for him in this way. He was gay, had always been gay, and would always be gay. *But God does love me,* Troy thought. *And so I'm going to love me, too.* He didn't need that subway seat anymore. He felt as if he could fly.

Troy has been sober for almost two years. He has a good job and good friends. He visits his mother often, and he is working on forgiving his father. Weekly Sexual Compulsives Anonymous meetings are a large part of his life. Occasionally, he buys a hot meal for a homeless person. The bottle of Kahlua sits on the shelf collecting dust. Troy keeps it as a reminder of how close he came to ending his life on Earth, and of how he came to know at last that he is always in God's grace.

Have you ever had a thought just pop into your head? Has an idea ever occurred to you "completely out of nowhere"? If this has happened to you at a time of your own deep searching or dark despair, I'm willing to bet that you've had your own conversation with God. If the thought or the idea was a positive, heart-opening, joyous one, then I *know* that you have.

One of the questions people ask often is, "How can I tell when I'm receiving a communication from God, and not just a random thought from who-knows-where?"

The answer is found in the very early pages of the very first book in the *With God* series. Said God:

> Mine is always your highest thought, your clearest word, your grandest feeling. Anything less is from another source.
>
> Now the task of differentiation becomes easy, for it should not be difficult even for the beginning student to identify the Highest, the Clearest, and the Grandest.
>
> Yet will I give you these guidelines:
>
> The Highest Thought is always that thought which contains joy. The Clearest Words are those words which contain truth. The Grandest Feeling is that feeling which you call love.
>
> Joy, truth, love.
>
> These three are interchangeable, and one always leads to the other. It matters not in which order they are placed.

Thoughts of anger, of retribution, of bitterness, or of fear are not communications from God. Thoughts of worry, of frustration, of limitation, or of inadequacy are not communications from God. Neither are thoughts of nonacceptance, of judgment, or of condemnation.

Nor are *any* thoughts that reduce hope, end joy, diminish spirit, or constrain freedom.

I know that Troy's communication on that train came right from God, because it was a communication of unconditional love and total acceptance. Those are thoughts, those are communications, you can always believe.

But now, let us ask ourselves another question. Was it a coincidence that, in the same neighborhood where Troy had gone to continue his self-defeating lifestyle, programs were being offered that could provide him the tools to change it? Was it by mere chance that one of those programs—the only one being offered the day of his visit—dealt directly with Troy's core issue? Was it sheer luck that the building happened to be right across the street from the liquor store where he'd purchased what he intended to be an instrument of his demise?

Or was this a true Moment of Grace, linking to another on the train the next day?

Whenever events seem to be playing themselves out as if by design, it may just be that Someone Else is a playing a hand in things. . . .

Not every illustration of this is as dramatic as the stories of Gerry Reid or Troy Butterworth. Some are even a bit lighthearted . . . but still impactful. Just ask Kevin Donka.

10

And a Little Child Shall Lead Them . . .

Holidays and holy days are always difficult times if things aren't going well. Meant to be seasons of joy and gladness, they can bring sadness instead, as Troy's story—and the untold personal story of countless others—can illustrate. Yet, also as in Troy's story, these can be times of healing. For the heart can be opened more easily at any time that a people's traditions and culture bring them to a place of remembering the great secrets of life.

It could be Ramadan. It could be Rosh Hashanah. It could be Beltane. It does not matter. All traditions and all cultures have special days and times when their deepest wisdom and their highest happiness are openly expressed through commemoration and ritual, through song and dance, through familial gathering and the sharing of joy and the celebration of Life Itself.

Celebration wasn't exactly the mood in which Kevin Donka found himself at the start of one particular Christmas season, however. In fact, he was feeling very lonely, very separated.

If only they would understand! he thought to himself. *If only they would stop being so critical! If only . . .*

Some serious misunderstandings had developed in Kevin's family. His sister was hardly speaking to him. His brother was angry, too. Even his father had joined the fray—and not on Kevin's side. And while Christmas was not a time to be arguing, Kevin reflected sadly, it was hard to ignore the feeling that his family had made some very unfair judgments about him.

It all had to do with a business agreement he'd entered into with his brother-in-law. Somehow, everyone had concluded that Kevin wasn't living up to his end of the bargain.

If only they would listen! Kevin thought now. *I'm the only one who's being fair about this,* he told himself bitterly. *I'm the only one. I'm the ONLY ONE!*

He was angry. In fact, during the week before Christmas it was just about all he could think about. He had almost decided not to take his own family to his father's house for the annual Christmas holiday gathering.

"I was distraught," he remembers. "I didn't know what to do or how to heal the disagreements between us. And I didn't want to go over there and have all that tension in the air, especially with the kids around. Kids can tell, you know. You think they don't know what's going on, but they know. They can feel it. I didn't want all of that spoiling their Christmas."

Kevin tried everything he knew to get past his feelings. He'd been reading, at the time, a book called *The Four Agreements* by Don Miguel Ruiz. Now he tried to apply one of the four agreements for healthful living mentioned in the text: Never take anything personally.

"It was hard," he says. "It's a great agreement to make with life, but it's hard when it's your own family that's being so judgmental, so critical of you. I thought they knew me better than that."

Kevin Donka is a chiropractor in Lake Hills, Illinois, and has healed many people there. But now, he mused ironically, he could not even heal himself. Of course, this was a sadness of the heart, not a condition of the body, he told himself, and so it was different. The way things were going, this would take some divine intervention. Something much larger than anything they taught him in chiropractic school.

Then came the Saturday before Christmas. Dinner at the Donka home was normal, if subdued. Kevin knew he'd have to make a final decision soon—and tell his family about it. How would he explain to his own children that they weren't going to see "Grampa" on Christmas Day? How could he share with his wife, Cristine, the depth of his bitterness?

"Daddy, Daddy, come watch me!" six-year-old Mariah squealed with delight as everyone settled down in the family room after dinner. Her green eyes sparkled, and her soft, straight brown hair swayed as she moved to the music of Britney Spears. She'd been practicing a song with her portable CD player all day. "Can you video me, Daddy?" She begged. "I want to watch it later and see how I'm doing!"

Kevin smiled. Children bring such joy. And his mind was diverted, if only momentarily, from his darker thoughts. So the two went downstairs to the larger space that in Kevin's youth would have been called the "rumpus room." There, he took out the video camera, found a good position on the sofa, and pointed the lens at Mariah as she started her routine all over again.

In the song Britney Spears sings, there's a line that goes: "My loneliness is killing me." But Kevin noticed that Mariah sang it differently. Mariah sang, "My onlyness is killing me."

"Sweetie, that's not what she says," Kevin gently corrected his daughter. "Those aren't the words." And he told her how the actual lyrics went.

Mariah thought for a moment. Then she said, "I like it better my way!"

Kevin shrugged, smiled, and they began taping again.

This time, now in the mood to tease her father, Mariah did something straight out of her six-year-old impishness. When she came to the line on which her Dad had corrected her, she sashayed toward the camera, put her face directly into the lens, and sang right to Kevin: *Your onlyness is killing you, Daddy!*

Kevin blinked from his side of the lens, then snapped bolt upright. "I felt as if I'd been hit by a two-by-four," he remembers.

His feelings of separation from his family of origin seared through his soul. His own words came back to him. *If only . . . if only . . . I'm the only one . . . .*

Then he knew that he'd received a message from a place far distant from both he and his little girl Mariah—and yet, existing right there inside of them.

Later that night, as he lay in bed, he picked up another book that he'd been reading—*Friendship with God*. After just a few pages, he turned to Cristine.

"I have to tell you about something that happened tonight," he said, and related his experience with Mariah and the song. "I think it was God talking to me about all this stuff with my family. It says in this book that God talks to us all the time. We just have to be open to it."

"I know," his wife agreed softly. "So, what are you going to do about it?"

A tear traced a path to Kevin's mouth, and he tasted its saltiness. He remembered the two questions from the *With God* books that he'd memorized.

Is this who I really am?
What would love do now?

"I'm going to go over there on Christmas Day and love them, no matter what they are doing and saying."

Cristine smiled.

The next day, Kevin called his father.

"We'd like to bring the family over for Christmas, Dad, if that's all right with you. I'd like to get past all this stuff that's between us. Let's have a nice holiday."

His father didn't even pause. "That's what I want, too, Kevin," he said.

And Kevin's *onlyness* wasn't killing him anymore.

It is from the mouths of babes that we so often receive our greatest wisdoms, and the case of little Mariah Donka is a wonderful and heartwarming illustration. Feelings of being alone against the world are very common. What is necessary to overcome this condition, as Kevin did in the experience above, is a moment of greater awareness. Sometimes the strangest things can startle us into that awareness. Like the innocent, seemingly unrelated, statement of a child.

But *was* Mariah's statement unrelated? Did it really have nothing to do with what was going on in her father's life at that moment? Was it simply the chance utterance, the naïve outburst, of a rambunctious, playful little girl? Or was this a case of Divine Intervention, of the most surreptitious kind? Could this have been a conversation with God?

I believe it was. In fact, I *know* it was. And I think that God speaks to us through the mouths of children often. Why? Because children have not forgotten. Children have not been "away" long enough to have lost touch with the deepest truth and the highest reality.

I am reminded of the story I told in *Conversations with God, Book 1* about the little girl who sat at her kitchen table one day, busy working with her crayons. Her mom came over to see what it was in which she was so engrossed.

"What are you doing, honey?" she asked.

The little girl looked up, beaming. "I'm drawing a picture of God!"

"Oh, that's so sweet," her mom smiled, "but you know, honey, nobody really knows what God looks like."

"Well," said the little girl, "if you'll just let me *finish* . . . "

You see how it is with children? It doesn't even occur to them that they cannot know what other people in the world—the so-called smarter adults—have no idea about. Not only are children totally clear, they do not judge themselves for saying what they think. Children just blurt out the truth, drop their wisdom, and dance away.

My wonderful friend Rev. Margaret Stevens tells a story on herself of a moment she says she will never forget. She had given her little girl a gentle swat on the bottom and a stern talking-to for something the child had done. When her daughter began to cry, Margaret looked at her and said, "It's okay now, I forgive you."

Her daughter looked straight at her and said, "Your *words* forgive me, but your *eyes* don't."

That's a stone-cold, dead-on insight. It's the kind of thing that only a child could see, and only a child could say, so clearly.

Margaret, today in her eighties, still uses that moment as a teaching tool in her talks and sermons, describing how her own child brought her a lifelong lesson about forgiveness, and that it must not be just lip service, but come from the heart.

And now, here in this story, Kevin Donka receives a teaching, too—this particular wisdom transmitted "by accident" through the mixed-up word of a little child. But *was* it a mix-up? *Was* it an accident?

Again I say, no.

Nor was it an accident that God told *me* this story, through Kevin. For this teaching was meant not only for the Donka household in Lake Hills, Illinois, but for the many thousands of people who will come to these words here, in this book.

Now I want to tell you that the teaching is larger than you might think. For as I pondered the lessons in Kevin's story, I realized that there was more here than meets the eye. I saw clearly that *"onlyness"* is a *spiritual condition*. It can be nonbeneficial or *beneficial*, depending upon which way we experience it.

If we understand *onlyness* as meaning that we are separate from everyone else—the "only one" doing this or that, the "only one" having a particular experience—then *onlyness* will be debilitating.

If we understand *onlyness* to mean that we are united with everyone else—that there is no one but "us," that we are all One—then *onlyness* will be enlivening.

We are either made bigger, or we are made smaller, by our understanding of *onlyness*.

Here is my understanding.

There is "only God" in the universe. There is nothing else. Now that is an extraordinary statement, of breathtaking implications. Among them: we truly *are* all One. We are made of the same stuff. Or, as eminent physicist Dr. John Hagelin puts it, "at its basis, everything in life is united. Life is a Unified Field."

Just how unified are we?

The world was shocked to learn in February 2001 that the genetic structure of human beings is 99.9 percent *identical*. Findings of the Human Genome Project undertaken by two separate teams of scientists around the world produced startling revelations about our species—evidence that finally gives scientific credence to what spiritual teachers have been telling us from the beginning of time.

Among the early conclusions of these scientific studies:

- There are far fewer human genes than anyone thought—probably a mere 30,000 or so, and not the 100,000 that most scientists had predicted. That is only a third more than those found in roundworms.

- Of those 30,000 human genes, only 300 have been found that had no recognizable counterpart in the mouse.

You've heard that there are only six degrees of separation between all human beings? Well, there are only 300 genes of difference between human beings and Mickey Mouse.

The more we find out about our world and how it is, and about life and how it works, the more we discover that we do live in a universe of what beautiful little Mariah called *onlyness*. Life is the only thing there is. All we will see as we discover more and more about it are mere variations on a theme.

I call that theme God.

What evolution invites us to do is to shift our thinking about *onlyness*, to end the *onlyness* of separation, and begin the *onlyness* of unity.

When we truly see that Life is the Only Thing There Is, then we will see that Love is the Only Thing There Is also. And so, too, will we see that about God. For Life, Love, and God are the same thing. These words are interchangeable. You can exchange any one for any other in virtually any sentence without altering the meaning or reducing comprehension. Indeed, you will expand it.

Life, Love, and God are communicating with us in a hundred ways every day, sometimes through the voices of children, and sometimes through the whispers of a Friend Within. . . .

11

Our Friend, Who Art in Heaven . . .

"Things will be better in Seattle, kids. Just you wait and see."

Maria's mom sang the words as she drove the rickety old station wagon down the highway. The car's red paint had already begun to look a little faded back in Philadelphia, but now it was more dust-colored than red.

It had been a long trip, and little Maria Endresen was tired of looking out the window. She was even more tired of squabbling with her three much-older siblings in the car. Because they were much older, they always seemed to be picking on her. Maybe she should have just stayed back home with her dad and two older brothers. Being the youngest, however, Maria wasn't given a choice. When her mom had made the decision to strike out and find a better life with nothing but an old station wagon, four kids, and $200 in her purse, there was nothing to do but go along.

"Why Seattle?" Maria had asked her mom a hundred times. "It's all the way across the world!"

"That's why. It's as far away as we can get from Philly and still stay in the same country," her mother answered.

Now, after days on the road, the city at last came into view, Puget Sound looking gray and cold. Maria didn't have a very good feeling about what was going on. She wouldn't have put it that way if she'd talked about it, of course. She would have said, "Mommy, my tummy is nervous."

Time passed, but the feeling of unease did not.

Maria's mother had found a job right away. That was the good news. But it was in Chinatown, a bustling, strange place. People talked fast and funny; they always seemed to be in a hurry to go somewhere. The store windows were filled with strange-looking things—naked ducks and chickens hanging by their necks, unidentifiable vegetables, and dried-up-looking whatevers that kept Maria's stomach turning over. Making matters worse, the streets were often wet, and the sky was cloudy most of the time.

No one paid attention to a little girl hanging out behind the front desk of the old hotel where her mother was working. She felt like a stranger here. There was no one to talk to; there were no children around. Her brothers and sisters were in school every day. Some days during her lunch hour, Maria's mother would walk her down to the waterfront to feed the seagulls, but she was generally left to entertain herself in the dusty hotel lobby. Mostly, she just felt alone . . . and lonely.

By the time Maria was old enough for school, all the other kids were out of school and out of the house. Maria and her mother had moved to south Seattle. The house her mother had found was bigger than any place they'd ever lived before, but rather than make Maria happy, it seemed kind of spooky, especially with that dusty cellar full of cobwebs in all those dark corners. At least it was in a neighborhood with other houses like theirs, and other kids to play with.

Maria's mom took longer to get home from work now, the red station wagon having died long ago and the bus from downtown Seattle taking a circuitous route. After working all day and spending an hour on the bus getting home, Maria's mom was often too tired and cranky to spend much time playing with her daughter. Maria's loneliness at eight years old had already become a way of life.

Every morning, Maria got herself dressed and off to school. When she came home in the afternoon she was alone, so she watched a lot of television. The big, old house creaked and groaned, and even though it was still daylight, Maria never liked being there by herself. It was scary. She would often hang out at the corner store, looking at magazines and talking to whoever would come in and out.

One day Maria was feeling a little hungry, but, as usual, she had no money. She thought of just taking that candy bar she wanted. No one would see. She wouldn't get caught. And it was only a few cents worth of candy anyway. She slipped the chocolate bar into the big pocket of her purple coat. "That was easy," Maria smiled to herself.

It was so easy, and the satisfaction was so great, that Maria began stealing regularly. There was never any money for her to spend, and there were always things Maria could find that she wanted, so she learned to just take whatever it was that caught her fancy. The purple coat was perfect. It had large pockets and was big enough to hide anything under it that she wished.

Some days Maria would take things just for the fun of it. It had gotten that bad. It was not about taking things that she thought she needed, or a chunk of candy when she was hungry. Now it was about just taking stuff for the thrill of taking it. She never felt guilty.

One day Maria was returning home from the store, munching on a candy bar she'd just stolen. That's when it happened. That's when she had the experience that changed her life—and that continues to affect her life to this very day.

Is this who you are? Maria heard a voice say.

She stopped and looked around. There was no one close to her.

Is this who you wish to be?

Now the voice seemed to be coming from inside her head. Maria froze.

Wh-what . . . do you mean? she found herself replying inwardly.

Is this who you are? the voice asked again.

Then Maria understood. She wasn't afraid, nor was she ashamed. She just simply understood that the voice was asking her if taking candy bars and other things that didn't belong to her was the kind of thing she really wanted to do, if being a thief was who she wanted to be in her life.

The voice sounded friendly. There was no judgment, no accusation. Just a question. A question that Maria found natural to answer.

No, she thought, *I don't want to be a thief.*

She threw the candy bar into a nearby trash bin. She felt better almost immediately. Then she became aware of a sudden and powerful inner knowing. She had larger things to do, there was a higher purpose, in her life. It seemed to her as though there were something specific she had come here to accomplish, and that this . . . this *business of stealing* . . . was getting in the way.

Maria knew in that moment that she would never take anything that didn't belong to her again. She also knew something else in that instant. She knew that she was no longer alone! Having always been alone, Maria had always *felt* alone. Now she did no longer. She knew she had a friend. She'd heard that friend's voice deep within her heart.

It would be some time before Maria would give this friend a name (she ultimately chose to call this presence in her life "God"), but on this day her loneliness fell away, and her "friend" became her constant companion.

Friendship with God is much more than a fanciful idea. It can be a functioning, actual reality. In the book *Friendship with God*, we are given seven steps that can lead us to that state of being. But it is not necessary to take such a route step by step. As in all processes of evolution, many steps—sometimes *all* of the steps—can be leapfrogged. In truth, when this happens it is not because we have skipped steps, but, rather, because we have simply taken them all at once.

That is what happened to Maria when she was a young girl. She had a mystical experience, a Moment of Grace, on a street corner in south Seattle, and it changed everything about the way she was experiencing her life. No longer did she feel alone. No longer was she confused about her values.

On that street corner, Maria and the universe scrunched together all of the steps in achieving a friendship with God, taking them all at once.

The Seven Steps to Friendship with God are easy to remember, and easy for us to take. They are:

1. Know God
2. Trust God
3. Love God
4. Embrace God
5. Use God
6. Help God
7. Thank God

Friendship with God discusses these steps in great detail. It talks about how life works out in the process of life itself. It actually illustrates that. It explores the Five Attitudes of God (listed later in this book, in chapter 15), and it explains the Three Core Concepts of Holistic Living (Awareness, Honesty, Responsibility).

It is an extraordinary document, and I would urge everyone to examine its contents thoroughly, to probe its statements deeply, to mine its treasures. If you do, you will see that in order to know someone, truly know them, you have to forget everything that you thought you knew about them, and everything that someone else has told you about them, and simply move into your own experience.

The same is true with God. You cannot truly know God if you think that you *already* know all there is to know about God—particularly if what you think you know is based on what other people have told you.

(Troy Butterworth offered us a striking example of that earlier. Other people, including a minister, told him what God thought about gays, and so he thought he knew God pretty well on that score. He was going straight to hell, and that was that. Then he moved into his own experience of God, and realized that God's love was unconditional and did not embrace the petty judgments that some human beings embraced—and that some human beings wanted others to believe that *God* embraced.)

You may find it very difficult to trust someone that you do not really know, and you may have the same difficulty trusting God.

You may find it very difficult to love someone that you cannot trust, and you may have the same difficulty loving God.

You may find it very difficult to heartily embrace someone, bringing them richly into your life, if you do not love them, and you may have the same difficulty embracing God.

You may find it very difficult to use anything in your life if you are unwilling to even hold it, to embrace it, and you may have the same difficulty using God.

You may find it very difficult to give much help to anyone for whom you have absolutely no use, and you may have the same difficulty giving much help to God.

And you may find it very difficult to feel gratitude in your heart for someone to whom you cannot give the slightest help, and you may have the same difficulty feeling gratitude for God.

As with all wonderful processes and revelations that

have been given to us in the *With God* series of books, one thing leads to another. It is also interesting that with the Seven Steps to Friendship with God, the entire process may be reversed. That is, you can begin moving toward friendship with God by first thanking God, for anything and everything in your life.

After taking inventory and seeing all for which you have to be grateful, it will follow naturally that you will want to help God. God is "up to" something, which you will soon discover if you but look into things even a little, and it will become quite natural for you to want to "help" God, to play your part in the Perfect Unfoldment of Your Self—which, it turns out, *is what God is "up to."*

Through the process of helping God, you will discover that what you are really doing is using God and all that God is. Through your use of God and all that God is, you will realize that you have truly embraced God in your life. In the moments of your realization that you have embraced God, you will quite naturally fall in love with God. In your great love for God, you will come to trust God implicitly. And when that whole process is finished, you will realize that you have come to know God as you have never known God before. You will have a very real, a very genuine, *friendship with God.*

And so we see that in this process the dominoes can fall either way. Or, as we observed earlier, they can all fall at once, as they did for Maria Endresen when she was a little girl.

Maria still has a friendship with God. It is not a figment of her imagination; it is not a flight of her fancy. It is very real, it is very genuine, and it is very practical. When Maria is at any kind of crossroads in her life, when she is approaching any choice point, when she is confronting any problem, when she is faced with any challenge, she knows that she is not alone. She has a friend. One who gives her advice.

It is always good advice.

Whispered in her heart.

12

Journeys of the Soul

Jason Gardham's unusual experiences began when he was a child. Always the first one out of bed in the morning, he loved living on a farm, where he could run and play and roam freely. His favorite place was a nearby forest, which bordered the family property. Every summer morning, after gulping down a sandwich, he would head for the woods.

His mother always knew that Jason was up and gone before anyone else in the family because she would come downstairs to find the peanut butter jar still sitting on the counter, the loaf of bread opened and left askew.

Jason went to the woods to play with his special friends. They weren't of this world, and Jason knew it, but he talked about them as if they were. When he entered the trees as the sun began to climb in the sky, he could feel the energy in the air and he would know right away if this would be a day when he would find the children jumping and laughing among the ferns. Sometimes they would be waiting for him, and all day they would hide behind trees and chase each other, laughing and running.

Other days, Jason would spend the morning looking and listening for them, but never finding them. On those days he would come home dejected and tearful.

"What's wrong, darling?" his mother would ask.

"My beautiful children aren't in the woods today. I don't know where they are," he would sob. That's what he always called them. His beautiful children.

Putting her arms around her little boy, Jason's mother had no inclination to doubt him, nor did it ever occur to her to chide him for conjuring up imaginary playmates. Once, when she simply asked him about them, and how he knew they were there, he'd replied, simply, "trust." And so, as he trusted his playmates, and life itself, to bring them to him, so, too, did she trust whatever he told her of his unusual experience.

Many times her son had matter-of-factly shared in detail the things he had seen or heard, things that might alarm most mothers. She had simply come to trust that her son was special somehow, that he was different.

In the space of such acceptance and unconditional love, Jason grew into a healthy, well-adjusted young man. And, having been given the freedom to experience unusual things and talk about them openly without fear of being mocked, he continued to do so. His mother had taught him that she, too, could be trusted.

Thus it came to pass that, at seventeen, Jason Gardham took a trip to the farthest reaches of the cosmos, just on the edge of heaven. And he did it without ever leaving his bedroom.

Now it must be emphasized here that we are talking about a normal teenager—hurting when he didn't get the girl, playing sports, developing his artistic talents. This is not someone who spent his time with drugs, or experimenting with acid trips. Books were more his style. Reading a good book was what he enjoyed.

One evening in July 1958, after finishing dinner, that's exactly what Jason decided he wanted to do. That's not what he *did*, but it is what he *wanted* to do. When he went to his room to find a book, he found instead a completely altered reality.

Stepping through the doorway, he found himself in total darkness. *Total* darkness. Not a light seeping in from any-where. *Whoa,* he thought, and reached for the light switch, when all at once he felt as if he were being rushed through a void at terrifying speed.

I'll die, his mind screamed. *There is no air here! I'm going too fast.*

Then he knew what he had to do. He had to trust. That's what he always did when strange things happened. So he called out to God. It was perfectly natural for him to do so. He'd always remained open to matters of the spirit and con-sidered himself to have a close, personal relationship with God. The support and guidance he believed he received through that relationship was an important part of his life. His faith, his trust, never wavered. He always believed that God loved him and was there for him always. He went to that place of trust now.

Immediately Jason experienced himself embraced, enveloped, by a marvelous feeling of perfect safety. It was a warm feeling, a feeling of utter peace and deep calm. As his heart gradually stopped racing, he gazed in wonder around him.

He was flying through the air! The blackness had been replaced with a breathtaking spectacle of stars and planets and moons and asteroids and comets and all the stuff of outer space.

Have I lost consciousness? Is this my imagination? he wondered.

As he watched the stars race by, he gazed with awe at the incredible beauty through which he was traveling at an unfathomable speed. On and on he traveled, feeling neither heat nor cold, aware only of the stars gliding silently past.

He thought, *Where I am going, and why am I being taken there?*

Then, again, he remembered God's love. He remembered: trust.

Instantly Jason felt himself slowing. And then, he stopped. Before him stood what seemed to be a wall—a huge *golden* wall, glowing with an unearthly light. It was so high that he couldn't see the top of it, and neither could he see its end to the left or right. Its beauty was awesome, and Jason could not believe his eyes.

As he hovered there, what looked like a bay window slowly took shape directly in front of him, its double panels opening. To Jason it felt like a window onto eternity, through which a soul could fly to heaven. Emanating from behind the window was an array of shimmering hues more brilliant, more spectacular than anything he had ever seen. Reaching out to touch the beam of colored light, Jason was forced to cover his eyes, for the light became so bright, and so beautiful, that he couldn't bear to look.

But I must look, he cried, and he felt his heart would burst with love.

Then he uncovered his eyes.

And was back in his room.

His return was as startling as his departure. Stunned, Jason stood in the place from which his body had never budged. He knew clearly—there was not a doubt in his mind—that he had been taken on a special journey. A journey of the soul, bringing him a glimpse of the largest reality. Call it God, call it heaven, call it what you will. Jason knew he had seen it, experienced it. *But why?* he wondered. *Why this journey?*

And then he thought that perhaps he might be wondering for a very long time.

He was right.

Oh, it wasn't that he didn't try to find an answer. He asked many people who he thought might have some clue that could explain what he had experienced. But their responses usually ran along the lines of, "It must have been something God wanted you to see, and when you're supposed to understand its meaning, you will."

And so, questions remained in Jason's mind. Sometimes the memory of his journey, and the feeling of not knowing exactly what it all meant, brought a tear to his eye. He felt sad for himself and his lack of awareness, but he felt even sadder for the world and the people in it who he feared would never know the wonder and the joy of what he'd experienced.

He would visit that memory, and retake that journey, in silent, private moments for almost thirty years.

Then in midsummer 1987, Jason happened to stop at a local art store to buy some supplies. He had just begun to browse when out of the corner of his eye he noticed a man coming toward him.

A very tall, imposing Native American with long, blue-black hair and dark, penetrating eyes, approached. He wore a waistcoat over a denim shirt. Three feet away from Jason he stopped, saying nothing.

At once Jason's being was filled with a thought. If a thought can fill one's whole body, permeating every cell, this is what happened to Jason. At the cellular level he knew: *This man has something important to tell you.*

He blinked past the feeling, forcing his attention back to the present encounter.

"Could I speak with you a moment?" the Indian asked in a deep, mellifluous voice.

Jason felt a twinge of nervousness. Then, he remembered. Trust.

"Yes," he replied evenly. "Of course."

"Perhaps we could step outside." Nodding, Jason followed him.

The two men took seats at an outdoor café next door. The stranger took a deep breath.

"I knew it was you immediately."

Jason blinked again, saying nothing. His heart pounded out his eagerness to know what the man had to say to him. But he felt paralyzed. He couldn't seem to find the words to pose the questions that were bubbling up inside him. While he was collecting his thoughts and preparing to ask who this American Indian assumed him to be, an image came to his mind. It was an image of the golden wall. And with the image came a feeling. Trust. Trust what is happening now. Trust your intuition. Just . . . trust.

Now Jason felt completely at ease. He knew that it was he who would speak first. It was he who would break the ice, make the communication easier, open the path for whatever the other man had come to say.

"Before you say anything, may I tell you about something? It's an experience that I had years ago, as a teenager. I somehow think you should know about it."

The American Indian smiled. "Please," he said. "I would like to hear."

Jason related the story of his trip through time and space. He didn't know why he was describing it. He just knew he had to do it. As he spoke he was careful to not leave out any details. He explained everything he had seen and felt, even expressing his sadness that he had never been given an understanding of the meaning of the experience. Somewhere in the middle of his narrative, he noticed a tear running down the other man's cheek.

Jason felt wonderfully unburdened when he finished. Now he knew why he'd told a total stranger his most intimate and personal story. He felt instinctively that he would finally be given a deeper understanding of what had happened to him three decades earlier. The man before him had the answers he'd been looking for. Jason didn't know how he knew that. He just knew.

The Native American spoke slowly.

"Let me tell you what I know," he said. Jason leaned forward in anticipation.

"I am Gary Winter Owen of the Maricopa tribe. I work here in the art store. One day, not many weeks ago, I was helping a customer when, suddenly, a feeling came over me that I should walk away from him and be alone. It made no sense, because we were having a perfectly fine interaction, but I could not shake the feeling. Finally, I excused myself and went into the storeroom in the back.

"It was then that I heard a voice in my head. It said to me, *Pick up a pen and write.* So, I did. I didn't know what I was supposed to be writing, so I just put down the first thing that came to my head. When I read what I had written, I did not understand it. Still, I knew it was important.

"Then the voice told me, *You will meet the man for whom this was written, and you will know him when you see him.*"

He looked right at Jason.

"I told my grandfather about this voice," he continued. "I showed him the message. My grandfather said that when I meet this man, I must come to know him, and learn from him."

Jason shifted uncomfortably. Gary went on. "I could not forget the message. It seemed such an important one, and so beautiful in its mystery. I fashioned a scroll and copied it there.

"Today, when I saw you . . . I heard the voice again."

There was a long pause. The two men's eyes met.

"It said to me that you were the one."

Jason released a breath. "I knew when I saw you that you had something to tell me," he said softly. "Something that I've been waiting to hear for thirty years."

Gary nodded. "It is true," he allowed. Then he handed Jason a beautifully fashioned roll of bark, tied with ribbon. One part of Jason did not want to open it, did not want to disturb its beauty. The larger part of him had to know what it said.

With shaking hands, he untied the ribbon. Looking up into the Indian's dark, almost black, eyes, Jason knew that he was being given a very special gift by someone who would become his friend.

He began reading the lavish, flowing calligraphy painted across the bark.

> *With honesty, integrity*
> *And loving in my soul,*
> *I took this man, this gentle man,*
> *into a wall of gold.*

Jason's heart stopped. He looked up at Gary, who simply smiled, then silently gestured with his head for Jason to read on.

> *A light so bright, it fills the night,*
> *a glow that angels know,*
> *for on the ground that we have found,*
> *a love begins to grow.*

Jason remembered the awesome, beautifully colored beam of light.

> *It rises high, solidifies*
> *with every smile and tear.*
> *And as we wait, we communicate*
> *To chase away the fear.*
>
> *We talk of life, we sing of strife,*
> *we share forgotten pain.*
> *And although we give, inquisitive*
> *is how we will remain.*
>
> *For I know not why, this man would cry.*
> *Your love is mine . . . behold!*
> *so I took this man, this special man,*
> *into a wall of gold.*

Jason put the scroll down. He knew then that he would never shed another tear of sadness at what he and others could not know fully. For he knew then that he *did* know—and that *everyone could know.* Life is joyous and, as always, is guided by God. And God's love was his to behold. Not only to behold, but to share.

Today Jason's life is infused with a deep sense of purpose, which carries him through his days. His self-appointed task is to bring peace and love to the world.

He seeks to do this by sharing one message. A simple message, but powerful.

Trust.

Trust yourself. For wisdom lies within you.

Trust each other. For we are all one.

Trust life. For it will surprise you, and delight you, and sustain you.

Trust God. For God loves you perfectly, and will help you all the days of your life, and will call you home when your work here is done.

Jason understands now that he is a teacher. And that Gary, a stranger in an art store, was to be his first student. But only his first. There would be many more, come to learn that there was nothing they *had* to learn. They only had to remember what they knew as children.

As beautiful children . . . dancing in the woods.

Was Jason's Journey real? Is it possible for human beings to "travel" to other realms? Can we actually leave our bodies—or, for that matter, remain with them—and experience alternate realities?

Says *Conversations with God, Book 2*:

> You are a Divine Being, capable of more than one experience at the same "time"—and able to divide your Self into as many different "selves" as you choose.
>
> You are a being of Divine Proportion, knowing no limitation. A part of you is choosing to know yourself as your presently-experienced Identity. Yet this is by far not the limit of your Being, although you think that it is.

Yet, is there such a thing as a "window onto Eternity," through which we can gaze, and from which we can bring back memories?

The answer is yes. Resoundingly, yes.

I speak from experience.

On the evening of January 8, 1980, my then-wife and I had a terrific argument. No doubt it was my fault. It usually was in those days. I was not a very easy person to live with. I wanted to be. I deeply wanted to be. But I just couldn't seem to make it, to get across the finish line on that one.

I don't even remember today what the tiff was all about. I mean, that's how insignificant it was. Probably something about whose turn it was to take out the trash. Who knows? What I do remember is what happened next. It's something I will never forget.

Stomping out of the TV room on the lower floor of our split-level house, I left my wife in the middle of our heated discussion, dismissing her with a wave of my hand and disappearing into the master bedroom with a slam of the door.

I threw myself on the bed in utter frustration and then, staring at the ceiling, began to cry. *Jesus*, I thought, *why can't we just get along? What does it take for people to just get along?*

I'd already failed in two previous marriages, and I could not figure out what I was doing wrong. *What does it take?* I asked God. *What does it take to be happy?*

I turned my head into the pillow and whimpered, "Please, God. Help me. I don't want to be like this, a man who argues over nothing. Help me. Help me. . . . "

Exhausted, I found myself falling fast asleep. It was as if someone had pulled a plug and drained all the energy out of me. I just let go and felt myself sinking deeply into the mattress, into the pillow. I remember the last thought I had before fading out.

This is going to be the deepest sleep of my life.

It was.

Somewhere in the middle of it—it could have been an hour into it, or a minute, or half a night, I don't know—I was awakened by an odd sensation. I felt as if I was being sucked right out of the bed. Have you ever had the feeling that you were falling out of bed? Well, it was like that—only backward. *Upward*, not downward.

Let me see if I can explain it another way. Imagine a fly, sitting very still on a table. Now someone comes along with a hose attached to a vacuum cleaner and manages to cover the fly with the end of the hose. He says, "Okay, turn it on!" and someone turns on the vacuum. *The feeling that fly would have is exactly how I felt.* I was lying on my stomach, and I felt as if I'd been literally sucked up off that mattress in one split second. It took my breath away.

My eyes were startled open, and even more startled to see that I was hovering over my own bed, looking down on what appeared to be a huge lump of clay, shaped and carved and sculpted to look exactly like me. But it wasn't me, I told myself, because I was *up here, looking down.* Furthermore, the familiar form on the bed had no life in it. No life energy. It was lifeless.

My first major awareness on this adventure had just, in that moment, dawned on me.

My God, I am not that body! I said to myself. *I am this. THIS.*

I am this . . . entity, this . . . energy . . . that is now OBSERVING that body.

As elementary as that may now sound, at the time it was a great revelation to me. The impact of that revelation was enormous, no doubt because it was not simply some concept or some theory, it was something that I was *experiencing*, right then and there.

No sooner did I absorb this awareness than I found myself being turned around, so that I was facing the ceiling, and then, in a *whoosh*, I flew right through the ceiling and out of there.

Immediately I found myself in a dark place that seemed like a tunnel, and then I felt myself being pushed or pulled through that tunnel at insane speed. There was no feeling of fear during any of this, just a sensation of incredible speed.

Soon, up ahead, I spotted a tiny speck of light, and it was to this light that I now knew I was racing. The speck grew bigger and bigger, until I felt myself sort of *pop* out of the tunnel and shoot into the light itself.

Now here is something interesting. I was in the light, and yet I also seemed to be outside of the light, looking at it. I remember with great feeling that it was almost impossible to look at, because it was so beautiful.

I don't know how to explain how a light can be beautiful, because a light is a light, right? Except that this light was beautiful. Perhaps it had to do with the way it *felt*. I don't know. I just know that its beauty was something that I was not able to hold. I mean, it was too big, too glorious, for a human consciousness to hold. I felt small, embarrassed. I remember thinking . . .

No, not me. I am not worthy of being in this light. I am not worthy of seeing this. With all that I have done, with all the black marks on my soul, with all the times that I have failed myself and others, I am not worthy.

Then I felt ashamed, because my thinking about all those things made me remember them more fully. And I cried in my shame and my guilt. I shivered with tears. Why had I not done better? Why had I made the lower choice so many times? I was deeply sorry. More regretful than I can ever remember being. And then I was filled—in that very moment I was filled—with a feeling that I cannot describe. Whenever I search for words, there don't seem to be any that fit. As I think about it now, I want to say that it was as if I had been given peace, true peace, total peace, for the first time in my life. It felt as though some giant, gentle finger was tilting my head upward with a touch on my chin. And I heard these words rumble through my heart:

You are perfect, just the way you are. You are beautiful beyond description, and I love you without condition. You are my child, in whom I am well pleased.

I felt cradled, embraced, the light surrounding me now, floating me softly in its center. All sadness left me. Even regret disappeared. I felt healed, made whole. My soul filled with gratitude, my heart burst with love.

Then I was filled with my second awareness: *I will never be forgiven for anything that I do.* No matter how sad I am about any action or decision, no matter how regretful, I will not be forgiven. *Because forgiveness is not necessary.* I am a child of God, an offspring of the Divine, and I cannot hurt or damage the Divine in any way, for the Divine is utterly undamageable, unhurtable. I will be accepted, always, in the heart and home of God, allowed to learn through my errors, allowed to become more and more of Who I Really Am, by whatever process I choose, even if it means damaging myself and others. For myself and others cannot be damaged, either. We only think that we can.

The impact of that revelation was enormous, no doubt because it was not simply some concept or some theory, it was something that I was *experiencing*, right then and there.

Immediately upon receiving this awareness, I found myself in a third reality, swiftly surrounded by a million, nay, a hundred million, tiny . . . *particles of energy* is the only way I can describe them. They were everywhere. In front of me, to the left of me, behind me, to the right of me. They seemed to me like tiny cells, or globules, each with their own shape and color.

And the colors! Oh, my, the colors were strikingly, astonishingly, breathtakingly beautiful. The bluest blues and the greenest greens and the reddest reds and the most magnificent combinations and hues that I had ever seen. And that is saying a lot for me, for you see, I am color-blind. . . .

So, for me, this was a spectacular sight.

Now these cells of color were dancing in front of me and all around me. Dancing there, forming a shimmering blanket of beauty that covered everything—that *was* Everything.

I knew then that what I was seeing was the Essence of All Life. It was life in its sub-sub-sub-molecular form. In its smallest particles. At its basis. At its root. And now here is something fascinating that I witnessed.

As I watched these cells of magnificent color dance and shimmer before me, I noticed that they were changing! They seemed to blink on and off, to be swallowed into themselves and to reemerge, in a different shape and a different color. And as they changed shapes and colors, the cells all around them changed shapes and colors, too, in order to accommodate and complement them. And the cells around those cells did the same, as did the cells around *those* cells, and so on, on and on . . . and I realized that the whole thing was one constantly changing, always adapting, ever-interconnected jigsaw puzzle. A pulsating, vibrating mosaic of pure energy.

My being overflowed with a desire to touch these unspeakably beautiful particles, to become one with them. I wanted to merge. I wanted to melt into them. I do not know why. It was an inner calling, an inner desire, felt at the very root of me.

I tried to move forward, to get closer. But with each move I made, the mosaic backed away. I thought I would "sneak up" on it, fake a move forward and then, suddenly, dart to one side. It did not work. I could not fool the matrix. It understood my every move. It actually *predicted* them.

I just couldn't get closer, and I started to weep. The sadness of this rejection and denial was more than I thought I could bear. And then the sadness disappeared, abruptly, as I was brought my third awareness: I could not get closer to the energy because I *was* the energy! When I moved, *it* moved. Of course. I was already merged!

All things are One Thing. There is Only One Thing, and there is No Thing that is not Part of that One Thing.

The impact of that revelation was enormous, no doubt because it was not simply some concept or some theory, it was something that I was *experiencing*, right then and there.

Once again, as soon as I understood it, I was removed from that reality. I found myself now facing an enormous book. It looked as big as the biggest book I had ever seen. No, twice as big. Three times as big. It looked as big as one hundred Manhattan telephone directories glued together. And on each page—on *each page*—was enough tiny type to fill one thousand encyclopedias.

As I stood before this mountainous volume, the voice I heard while embraced by the light came back to me. It said in the gentlest way, almost indulgently, but not in any way making fun of me:

Okay, Neale, okay. You have searched your whole life for answers. You've looked and looked and your search has been real, it has been sincere, it has been an honest search for truth. So here. Here are the answers.

With that, the pages of the book flipped past me, as if fanned by some gigantic thumb, or blown by some holy wind. Quickly they flew past, the whole document exposed, page by page, within a nonnosecond. And yet, I was able to read and absorb every word on every page.

And then I knew. I knew everything there ever was to know, is now to know, and ever will be to know. I understood the cosmology of the universe and the secret of all of life. I saw the simplicity of it all. The utter and elegant *simplicity*.

The impact of that revelation was enormous, no doubt because it was not simply some concept or some theory, it was something that I was *experiencing*, right then and there.

That was my fourth awareness. And I remember saying, as the book's final page fanned past and the heavy back cover closed . . .

Of course.

That's all I said. Simply . . .

Of course.

I woke up then. I was back in my body, and it felt heavier than I had ever experienced it. It seemed as though one little finger weighed a ton. I wanted to reach over to the bed table and find a pen and paper so that I could write down what I had just experienced, so that I could remember it, so that I could prove that I'd had it. But I could not move my arm. It was all I could do to blink my eyes.

Then, one last time, I heard that voice, my Special Voice, which had been coming to me during this dream, this journey, this, this . . . what*ever* it was. And the voice said:

It is not necessary. Do you imagine that you will forget what has happened to you? Yet you cannot prove it, nor do you need to. The Truth can neither be proved, nor disproved. It simply is.

With that, I fell asleep.

I awoke the next morning in a state of euphoria. Dancing into the shower stall, I turned on the faucet and was hit with a blast of cold water, and I did not even mind. In fact, it felt spectacular, invigorating. Then I warmed the water and stood there, watching it cascade from the nozzle onto my body.

I felt that I was One with the water, One with the nozzle, One with the tiles of the shower stall. I felt that I was One with everything, and I imagined that this is what it must be like to be on hallucinogenic drugs. I spread the fingers of my hand and pressed my palm against the wall—fully expecting it to go right through the tiles, because I could *see the molecules of the tile and the molecules of my hand,* and I realized that walking through walls was merely a matter of placing my solid matter where the solid matter of the wall *was not*. This would be easy for anyone with *insight*. That is, the ability to *see in*.

I continued to soak in the shower, and I fought, then, to remember what I had read, what I had seen, in the book. I called it the Big Book, and I was struggling now to remember even a single word that I had found there.

Then the voice said to me . . .

You are not to know.

. . . and I was caused to understand that if I were to try to carry around in my conscious mind all that I had been allowed to see, I would "fry" my circuits. It would be just too much, how to say this . . . *electricity* . . . too much *energy* . . . to hold in a small space of physicality such as my brain.

Then I was told:

Simply know that you know. And know that everyone else knows, too. And that all you have to do when you need to remember a particular thing in a particular moment is to call upon the wisdom within you. You will remember.

The feeling that left me with was too incredible to even describe. I stood in that shower for twenty minutes and it felt as if I was aware of every single drop of water that hit me. When I got out, the cooler air from the other side of the curtain greeted my body. It felt like I'd had a bottle of fresh, sparkling life poured over me. I was tingling and my psyche was wide open. I remember drying myself off and thinking how extraordinary it was that I could sense every fiber in that towel.

Everyone at work that day wondered what I was "on." One person stared at me when I arrived and finally said, "What happened to you? You look twenty years younger." I said, "I do?" And she replied, "You should see your face."

The feeling of being "in this world, but not of it" stayed with me for weeks, fading slowly as time went on, but hanging around at some level for quite a while. And for all the years since that day, up to this very moment, I can recapture that feeling, and the tearful joy of that experience, by simply recalling it.

It is mine to keep, it is mine to have and to hold, it is mine to reexperience whenever I wish. The Voice was right. I will never forget it.

And so what I can tell you from experience is this: Journeys of the soul, such as that taken by Jason Gardham forty years ago, are not only possible, but occur all the time. All of us take them. All of us. For not a single soul remains with a body, without release, from physical birth until physical death.

When a soul does leave a body, either during sleep, during what some people call a "trance," during a meditation, or simply for a moment during a walk in the woods (or stepping into a bedroom), there is nothing to be afraid of and nothing to worry about and nothing to be embarrassed about or reluctant to talk about with another.

In fact, it is good to talk about it with one another. For these are Moments of Grace, and as we share our experience of them, we touch the world with their wonder and their magic and their power to change lives.

Like the life of John Star, who had a very interesting experience one day on the shores of Lake Michigan. . . .

13

The Land of Shadows

John Star sat at the kitchen table, his head in his hands, his cold breakfast still on the plate before him.

"Not much of an appetite this morning, John?" asked his mother. For the past few days she had noticed John moping around the house. It wasn't like him to be so listless.

"Mom, I can't seem to get a grasp on things." John decided to confide in her a little, even though he didn't want to worry her. "I don't seem to be going anywhere. And I am lately haunted by these questions going round and round in my head. Big questions . . . like, what is really important? Why am I here? Where did I come from?" He looked up at his mother beseechingly. "I don't understand why I'm so restless, and yet I don't seem to have much energy."

She sat down beside him, "Honey, these are questions we all grapple with, all our lives. You have to give yourself some time. After all, you just graduated from high school. You have the summer to mull these things over. It will just take a little time for you to work out all the reasons why. And remember, most people never find those answers."

John sighed. Dear Mom, he thought, she means well. But that wasn't really helping him all that much. His mother suddenly brightened. "Why don't you go for a swim? You know that always makes you feel better."

John thought, sure, why not? Nothing else to do. Might as well get some exercise.

Lake Michigan was warm this time of year. Today, under the cloudy sky, the water looked more gray than blue. John was a good swimmer. He'd been comfortable in the water since he was a child, having competed for years on the city swim team. He liked to go out into the lake past the breakwaters, about a half mile offshore where the water was cooler and clearer.

As he began a smooth, freestyle stroke, cutting through the water at a fast and even speed, he felt himself enter that state of consciousness he had always found so soothing . . . not thinking about anything, just becoming one with the water, gliding through without thought, propelled only by the strength of his arms and legs, seeing nothing but watery shapes and shadows beneath him. This is a place that athletes call The Zone.

But on this particular day, the water was choppy. As John turned his head to breathe, he inhaled an oncoming wave. It broke his concentration, and as he sputtered and tried to catch his breath, another wave caught him in the face. As strong a swimmer as he was, John knew he could be in trouble. He was more than a half mile from shore, and he realized suddenly that under these conditions he might have difficulty swimming. He turned around and headed back toward the shore.

John had gone only a few yards when his head began to buzz and he felt himself growing dizzy. Suddenly, he heard a loud snap behind his head. Without a warning, the water at once became smooth. John stopped stroking and looked up. The sky was clear and the sun was shining brightly; the lake had turned a deep blue.

What the heck is happening? John was puzzled as he gazed at the clear sky. The sun seemed brighter than usual, but he was able to look without his eyes hurting. Suddenly, he had the sense that he was being beckoned somehow. He looked down to see an unbelievable sight.

There below him was his body, still swimming toward the shore, moving as straight and fast as a motor boat. He watched in awe and wonderment. If that was him there, and his consciousness was here, where was he *really*, and what was happening to him?

A light seemed to be coming from behind him. It was a peculiar light, a light with . . . *feeling*. He turned toward it. It was delicious! It bathed him in the most wonderful warmth; John soaked it up like a sponge. A feeling of total freedom came over him in that moment. It was as if all the pressure of a lifetime had been released; the lid that had kept so much tension inside had been at last lifted. He could breathe again.

Energy seemed to flow into him, loosening and softening parts of him that he hadn't even known existed. His whole being thrilled to the most wonderful, joyful feeling. He knew that somewhere, sometime, he had known this feeling before, but he could not remember when. It was like . . . *coming home*.

Time itself seemed to be softening. For as long as John could remember, the minutes, days, and years of his life seemed to be fixed, like the markings on a ruler. Now the measuring stick of time was becoming soft and flexible. It seemed to stretch and shrink, like a rubber band.

He could see events of his past, examine them with greater clarity and in more detail than when they originally occurred, and linger with these memories for an unlimited time. But then, it seemed as if no time at all had gone by.

Back and forth John went, deep into episodes of his history, then returning to the light. Or was it that the world he had known was receding? The life that he had come to assume was the only life there was . . . the certainties, the doubts, the pride and guilt, the pleasures and fears . . . they were all fading away. The only thing that remained was the light and the awesome feeling of well-being that the light contained.

It felt as if he was waking up, as if he had been in a deep sleep, dreaming an intense and detailed dream, and now he was alert and the dream was fading away.

As his eyes slowly became adjusted to the brilliant radiance, John could make out shapes in the light. There were people standing around him! People whom he knew and loved. What's more, the place where he found himself was completely familiar.

"Are you having a nice trip?" asked one of his friends. The others broke out into roaring laughter. They were making a joke. John intuitively understood that they were asking him about his earthly sojourn, and he joined them in their laughter.

How good it felt to laugh so freely! He was totally alive again, with a life that was beyond beginning and end, a life that was eternal.

The cosmic world that he had entered was now as solid and real as the world that he had left behind, but the light was still visible. It was a living light. It had vitality and feeling. It was focused in every living thing, just as the sun can be focused to a point with a magnifying glass. There were colors, too. Not only the colors that he was familiar with on Earth, but a palette of colors, some that he'd never seen.

Surrounding all his friends and every other living thing was color, arranged in intricate geometrical patterns, each pattern unique, every pattern original. Permeating the colors and patterns was sound—countless octaves of sound. It was as though the colors could be *heard*. It was very subtle, practically imperceptible, but reaching to infinity.

Superimposed on this vast life-giving hum was the melody that was created by the individual sound of every living thing. Light and sound and color and geometrical patterns were all combined into a totality of harmonic perfection.

Years may have gone by. Years or hours or minutes, there was no way to know. Be-ing was the only reality. Be-ing, which was inseparable from the moment, inseparable from the eternal *now*, inseparable from the life that was in all other beings.

Even though this place was as solid and real as the world he left behind, time and space were not an obstacle. It was a place where there were no opinions, conclusions, or beliefs, a place where there was only awesome beauty and joy.

Then, images of John's other life began to flicker in his mind—fleeting at first, but growing stronger and clearer. Visions of people who were dear to him came into focus, visions of things he wanted to see and do. Finally, from somewhere deep within him, a powerful voice welled up:

> *You have seen enough of eternity.*
> *It's not yet time for you to stay.*
> *Return now to the Land of Shadows*
> *Where the mortal creatures play.*

Whooshshsss, whooshshsss. John raised his head to see what was making that sound. Tiny wavelets were breaking along the edge of a mirror-still lake, rattling the small pebbles that lined the shore. He was lying in the sand on the shore of Lake Michigan, just a few inches from the water. He felt incredible, as if he'd just had the best rest of his life. He rose to his feet and looked around.

To the west, John could see the Chicago skyline, reflecting in the lake, silhouetted by an awesome red-orange sun. The sky was a deeper blue than he had ever remembered seeing it, the trees greener. It was as though a veil had been lifted from his eyes. He could have been gone for years, or a moment. Like a man who had lived a long, full life and had returned to the place of his youth to gaze again upon the once-familiar scenery, he saw that everything was the same, yet different somehow.

Was it all a dream? he wondered. *Or did I see what it is like to be really, truly awake, and am I dreaming now, once again?* Somehow he knew the answer.

He headed for home, the breeze chilling him in his wet swimsuit, no longer wondering about his place in the world. John had seen his space in the cosmos, and it was perfect.

He walked through the back door and found his mother puttering in the kitchen.

"Hi, Mom," he chirped.

"Hi, honey. How was your swim?"

"Cosmic!" John answered with a wide grin. "Cosmic!"

What was amazing to me when I first heard John's story is how similar it was to Jason's, and to mine. Each "visit" to "the other side," or "a larger realm" or whatever you want to call it, brought visions of an incredibly beautiful, awesome light and spectacular colors.

John and I both saw energy in the form of geometrical patterns, each pattern unique, each pattern original. John also experienced *sound* with the energy patterns, something that others have also reported. It has been long suggested by mystics that the sound of *Om* is the signature sound of the universe, of Life Itself.

What I always come back to when I hear about experiences like these, or remember my own, is the first major message that I received in the over 1,500 pages of the *With God* books: We are all one.

Everyone and everything is made up of the most exquisite building blocks you could ever imagine. I have seen that

Oneness. I have experienced it. Yet you don't have to have seen it to hold it in your reality. You merely have to feel it in your heart, and to embrace it in your soul. And that is easy to do. That is a decision, not a reaction. Like love. Love is a *decision*, and most people think it is a reaction.

Another thing that struck me about John's experience was a knowingness that came over him that "be-ing was the only reality." This is in beautiful harmony with the last of the three declarations made by *CWG, Book 1:*

1. We are all one.

2. There's enough.

3. There's nothing that we have to do.

All there is, is to Be. The difference between "beingness" and "doingness" is like the difference between night and day. Most humans are deeply involved in "doingness" lives. They are running around doing this and doing that, doing this and doing that, and all they wind up with is a great big pile of do-do.

We are going to be seeing on this planet in the next fifty years a new kind of human, a New Human, who will not come from "doingness," but who will come from "being-ness" in every moment. Many people are making this trans-formation even now. It is quite possible to do so, even in the workaday world. You don't have to go off and live in a cave for twenty years, or meditate nine hours a day, or any of that. Not that those are bad things to experience. It's just that they are not necessary.

It is not necessary to become a recluse, to "drop out," in order to feel the bliss of Beingness expressed in, as, and through you. You can experience this feeling as you perform your work in the world, in fact, *because* of the work you do in the world.

You can even use the process of moving into Beingness as a tool in finding Right Livelihood. All you have to know is what it is you want to "be." That is, what state, or states, of being do you wish to experience and express in, as, and through you? After you make this choice, you simply reject any kind of activity in the world (and certainly any kind of occupation) that does not cause you to express this.

A small book which can be read in forty minutes, *Bringers of the Light*, explains how this process works, specifically, and how it can place a person in the job of their dreams, creating Right Livelihood at last. I wrote this little book in answer to hundreds of requests from people all over the world who had read about Beingness in the *Conversations with God* books and wanted to understand more about it.

There are thousands of stories of people who have experienced Beingness through journeys out of the body, like the stories told by Jason, myself, and John. Perhaps you know of someone who has lived such a moment. Perhaps you, yourself, have. I have included these stories here so that people who have had such experiences may cast away any lingering feelings they may have been carrying around that they are somehow weird or abnormal. These kinds of experiences, I want to say again, are very common and *quite* normal.

Yet not all Moments of Grace arrive on the doorstep of our soul in such spectacular packages. Some come hidden in tiny boxes. I wouldn't want you to feel left out, thinking that you've never had a true Moment of Grace in your life, if you have not had one of those Thunderbolt Experiences.

People who have the kinds of experiences Jason and John and I have described here are no more special than anyone else—although they may be just a little more inquisitive! Truly, I often wonder if it is the person who asks endless inner questions about cosmic realities who draws to him or herself the brand of Moments of Grace that we are talking about here. Yet that is not the only brand, nor is it guaranteed to be the most effective. Many people have come back from such inner journeys with more questions than answers, and more confused than ever!

God finds many ways to create a Moment of Grace, and it does not take a thunderbolt experience to produce an electrifying result. The outcome of a Moment of Grace might be a huge life change, or a simple, gentle, insight. Both could have an enormous impact on how you live the rest of your days.

Let Margaret Hiller of Ashland, Oregon, tell you a little story in her own words. . . .

14

Seeing the Sacred in Every Moment

A great teacher taught me that the entire journey is sacred—no matter what it looks like. I call him St. Anthony. He is a little boy.

Anthony began his own journey in a very precarious way. He was born as a drug-addicted baby and his grandparents took custody and adopted him immediately, but the doctors said that it would take a miracle for Anthony to live.

"What do you mean, a miracle? What kind of miracle?" his grandmother asked.

The doctors told her that for this baby to live, someone would have to hold him virtually nonstop for the first two years of his life. It would take that long for the nurturing to "take," for the tiny body to heal.

Without hesitation, his grandmother said, "Well, heavens, I can do *that!*"

And she did.

Anthony lived with his grandparents in a wonderful environment. He was, quite literally, embraced by love and was given the gift of being with people who were deeply spiritual. From his first day on Earth, unconditional love and spirituality were part of his life. Naturally, he flourished in this atmosphere and was very happy. He could not know that for the second time in his young life there would be a drastic change—and a shift to a new family.

When Anthony was six, his grandmother became very sick with cancer and died. I was on his grandmother's support team while she was dying, spending many nights at her house, and much of that time was with Anthony. He was sad, of course, about what was happening, but his rich spiritual understanding—even at six—gave him an awareness that his grandmother was going to a wonderful place, and he could find a way to be happy for her.

A few months later his grandfather died also, and I often think it could have been of a broken heart. Now, this might have devastated some children, but, again, not Anthony. The incredible love he was given in his first years must have made him feel very secure in the world, because he came through this difficult time beautifully.

Immediately, his faith in the world was rewarded when we received word that his aunt and uncle had agreed to adopt him, even though they both had made a previous decision in their marriage to not have children.

Because of my closeness to all of these circumstances, I was privileged to make the trip with Anthony to meet his new family. I felt that I was delivering a wise, old soul, who would be a teacher to his new guardians. And Anthony kept teaching me. His questions and fears would open me to my own questions and fears, and together, we would find peace in our souls in the midst of a heartbreaking experience.

Our plane connected in Denver and the flight was late, so we got to experience that wonderful joy of running from one gate to the other and, of course, it was the farthest gate away.

I took Anthony by one hand and held our carry-on bags in the other and as we sprinted down the corridor, I yelled over to the ticket agents "Call the gate, please tell them to hold the plane." The ticket agents looked at me like I was nuts! And, of course, they didn't hold the plane.

Anthony looked up at my face (not an angelic countenance, I confess) and said, "Mawguet, are we having a wunning day?"

I said with great frustration, "Yes! That is exactly what we're having—a wunning day!"

We arrived just in time to watch the plane backing away from the gate. (You know the feeling—fun, right?) Anthony and I made our way to the ticket counter and learned that our next connecting flight would be in five—I repeat, five—hours.

My first thought (I wasn't really in my Sacred Self in that moment) was, *I've got to spend five hours in an airport with a six-year-old? God, are you kidding?* I could only imagine that the five hours was going to be "interesting."

And then, my lesson in It's All Sacred began.

The ticketing agent asked us, "Would meal vouchers help?" Anthony enthusiastically reached for the vouchers and thought this was as good as winning the lottery! I was fuming and Anthony was delighted as we ate our "happy meals," which took a grand total of half an hour.

We then made our way to a mostly empty waiting area . . . where we had four and one-half hours left to wait for the plane. I was not looking forward to this experience because I didn't really know what to do with a six-year-old and I forgot to ask, "What is God up to in this experience?" (It's the first rule in seeing the Sacred unfold in all life experiences.)

Anthony, though, was unaffected by the wait and proceeded to unload his backpack, pulling out all the Power Rangers, trail mix, coloring books, and crayons we had packed. He then made a large circle on the carpet with all of these "sacred elements," stretched out belly-down in the middle of the space, and began to color.

I thought to myself, *This will last about ten minutes.*

In fact, this sacred ceremony lasted for the next four and a half hours. And the story gets better.

Across the way in another waiting area, a little boy began to cry—the kind of wail that, no matter what the parents did, he would not be consoled. Anthony got up to look over at the wailing boy and with great enthusiasm motioned with his pointing finger for the boy to come over.

The little boy, still wailing, walked timidly across the hallway, under his parents' watchful eyes, and stood at the edge of the circle of stuff that Anthony had laid out. Anthony looked up inquisitively.

"Don't you have any coloring books?" he inquired.

Sniffling, the boy answered, "No."

Anthony, in a kind of surprised tone, said "Well!" and tore a page from his coloring book, slid it across the carpet along with a few crayons, and motioned for the little boy to enter the circle. (It's interesting to note that the boy did not enter Sacred Circle until he was invited.)

Anthony then asked the little boy, "How old are you, anyway?"

Through more sniffles, wiping tears with his sleeve, the little boy answered, "Three."

Anthony looked up at me, rolled his eyes, and whispered, "Figures!"

As the hours rolled by, other children found their way to Anthony's sacred circle, each one standing on the edge until they were invited to enter. The circle kept growing, the edges pushed out to make room for more arrivals.

Soon, parents began to gather, and as we witnessed this scene with amazement, we forgot about the books we were reading and our frustration over missed connections and late arrivals. We were propelled—that is a good word for an airport—into the sacred moment, the eternal moment where time does not exist, only love, only peace, only what matters.

I realized in that moment that I would never have those sacred hours with six-year-old Anthony again—that rare kind of opportunity, when we can see, and be present, with the Beloved, whatever the circumstance, whoever the Beloved may be.

That day I came to remember that *the entire journey* is sacred, that every experience has been meant for our instruction, for the unfoldment of sacred self, and for the celebration of who we truly are. "St. Anthony" helped me to remember this.

I am happy to report that Anthony's aunt and uncle, who, as I said, had never wanted children but were willing to try the idea, now consider their lives far more complete with Anthony. And this child is thriving! Emotionally, physically, mentally, spiritually thriving!

I wish everyone blessings on the journey—and remember to take your coloring book and crayons!

Remember, indeed.

I want to thank Margaret for sending me that story. She and her husband, David, are among those who have already accepted The Invitation. (I'll be telling you more about that at the end of this book.) Margaret and David go from place to place, from church to church, from hall to hall, from person to person, sharing their personal experience of small moments that contain large truths. What I call Moments of Grace.

There are lots of wonderful lessons in this story. The idea that every moment is sacred, and can hold for us wondrous treasures and great teachings, is one of them. Another is that when people (of any age) are surrounded by deep caring and true love, they are given incredible equipment with which to handle life's most challenging times.

A third one is: Be the source. That's a major message,

appearing over and over in the *With God* series of books. If there is something that you wish to experience yourself, be the source of it for another.

Now I don't think that young Anthony was doing this consciously (although, as spiritually aware as he is, I'm not so sure), but, apparently without knowing it, he was practicing this exact principle. He wanted to experience, I am sure, lack of fear as he headed for his new home, and when he saw a little boy across the aisle crying, he took that little guy's fear away and in the same stroke took away his own.

That's how the process works, and when you learn to do it consciously you've learned a great secret. If you want to feel happiness, make another person feel happy. If you want to feel companioned, and not lonely, be a companion to another and make *them* feel not lonely. When you want to experience joy, cause another person to experience joy. In fact, no matter *what* you want to experience, the fastest way to do it is to cause another person to experience it.

Do not wait for the world to bring you what you want. Be the source of it for another. That's what Anthony was doing there in that airport. I mean, what kid wants to be bored for four hours? So, he stops other kids from being bored. And guess who winds up being not bored. . . .

There's magic in this. This is a formula for magic.

Now there was at least one more lesson to be learned from this little story about Anthony.

Often when bad things happen to good people (and especially when those good people are children), we wonder why life has to be the way it is. We ask, "What's going on here?" We question the infinite love of the universe. Yet what I have come to understand is that there is a beautiful design being embroidered by the soul.

If we look at the embroidery from one side, all we see is a mishmash of crisscrossing lengths and colors that make no sense at all and might actually be called ugly. Looking at it from the other side produces an entirely different experience. We see the loveliness of the design, the wonder of its intricacy, the *necessity* of the mishmash.

Dr. Elisabeth Kübler-Ross, the eminent physician and psychiatrist and a pioneer in the field of grief and loss, death and dying, who has become one of the world's most beloved teachers, has a wonderful way of putting all this into context. She says:

"Should you shield the canyon from the windstorms, you would never see the beauty of their carvings."

I've never forgotten that.

The opportunity to have worked closely with Elisabeth as a member of her staff was one of the great Moments of Grace in my life. She has touched an entire world with her compassion, her deep understanding of the human condition, and her love for all of humanity.

Sometimes I am asked, "Are there angels on Earth? Do angels walk among us?" And I answer, "Yes! I know one!"

I consider Elisabeth Kübler-Ross to be an angel who has healed many lives.

And actually, David Hiller has had an experience that was an outgrowth of Elisabeth's work. It's a wonderful example of how the things we do can touch, by extension, thousands of others.

15

It's Never Too Late to Be Blessed

If you have ever had the experience of not feeling welcomed in some circumstance in your life, you know how devastating that can be. Many people hold onto that disappointment for a long time. For some, it still affects them to this day.

Until recently, David Hiller felt profoundly unwelcomed and in pain about an experience he had when he was nineteen years old. Then, just before his fifty-second birthday, a major shift took place in his life. He told me recently how it happened. Here is his story, in his own words. . . .

In June 2000, my wife, Margaret, and I were guest presenters at Unity Village in Kansas City, the headquarters of the Unity Church. We offered one of our healing workshops, which we present at churches all around the country, called *Shifting into Miracle Thinking.*

We were feeling really grateful to have supported and facilitated many people that day in their powerful healing shifts, but little did we know that later in the week it would be my turn to be healed. It happened when we attended another presenter's workshop.

Entitled *Coming Home*, the workshop was presented by a Unity minister, Sky St. John. In the midst of the session, Sky told us a story of how he was trained to do this workshop by Elisabeth Kübler-Ross.

During his training Elisabeth told a story that really touched Sky's heart (and when Sky retold the story, it also opened mine). Elisabeth's story went like this:

In one of her large workshop groups, which included a number of Vietnam vets, she asked those vets to go into another room so that she could explain a process concerning them to the remaining group. The vets left the room and waited until they were called back into the bigger group.

While the vets were gone, she told the rest of the group that it was time for some healing to take place, that these guys had been holding onto lots of grief, lots of feelings of not being supported or loved or welcomed when they came back to America from Vietnam, and it was time to begin to heal those wounds that were so deeply seated.

She asked this workshop group to cheer the vets on as if they were now coming home for the first time, to celebrate them in a loving, powerful, welcoming way, to whisper tender healing words, to give them lots of encouragement, and to bless the vets when they came back into the room—in other words, to welcome them home in a way that would touch them to the very core of their being. The workshop group agreed to do this and Elisabeth invited the vets back into the room.

As they arrived, the audience cheered and clapped, sang songs, and gave lots of loving encouragement and healing energy. The vets were so overcome with emotion that tears began pouring down their faces. They were filled with such powerful emotions that some fell to their knees, weeping. It was hard for many of them to contain the blessing of the welcome. And yet, they were so grateful to receive it. Someone began to play parade music at the piano, and a circle was created around all the vets.

Elisabeth asked the vets to walk around the circle and receive a personal message of blessing and welcoming from each person, and to be held and cheered. Some of the vets were so overcome that they could not walk. So, they crawled on their hands and knees around that circle as they experienced coming home in a whole new way. There wasn't a dry eye in the group. Everyone was touched by this healing ceremony. Not only did the vets receive healing that day, but everyone in the entire group was touched and blessed in that experience.

Sky told us this profound story in his compassionate, gentle way and shared that hearing Elisabeth's story had opened in him the immense need that we all have of being welcomed in our lives.

As he addressed our workshop group at Unity Village, you could feel the intense emotional desire he had to serve our group to also feel this profound support in an experience of Coming Home.

Sky continued to address our group and asked if there were any experiences in our lives where we did not feel welcomed and supported, whether it be by parents, by other people, or in whatever circumstance there might have been where we weren't acknowledged and supported for who we are.

He stated that in the Coming Home process we were being given an opportunity to transform the experiences of being unwelcomed into blessings, to heal those wounds once and for all—because there is powerful healing medicine in being welcomed. So those who wanted to receive the healing blessing of "coming home" were invited to gather in the back of the room. Everyone else stayed up at the front of the room.

There must have been at least 150 people who went to the front of the room to do the welcoming. I, being a workshop presenter at this conference myself, naturally started to walk up towards the front to be on the welcome team. But I heard a little voice in that moment that said to me, *David, you need to go to the back of the room. There are some things that are really important in your life that you haven't healed because you didn't feel loved and supported.*

The message was loud and clear and rang true, so I listened and trusted. I went to the back of the room, even though I didn't know what I would say when it came my turn to speak. I waited as each person went up to the microphone and spoke to the welcoming group, describing a circumstance where he or she felt unwelcome. The individual made statements to the "welcome team" like "you represent my parents, or my siblings, or my work colleagues," or whoever was a part of that person's story of not being welcomed.

And then, as soon as the person spoke, he or she would walk towards the front of the room as the welcome team began to cheer, applaud, and hold that individual, giving that Beloved lots of positive support. Sky would say, "You have come home," and it would touch that individual's heart with profound healing.

As I watched this exceptionally emotional experience for others, my turn was getting closer and closer. Uncertain about what I was going to say, I kept feeling that it was nonetheless very important for me to participate.

Soon, my turn came, and as I walked up to the microphone, I heard that same little voice say, *David, you were one of those Vietnam vets and you've held onto the memories and pain of this experience for many, many years. You weren't welcomed home. Your country forgot about you and it hurts to this day. Now is your chance.*

So, trembling, I walked up to that microphone and I took it in my hands and I choked out the words, "I was one of those Vietnam vets and my country forgot about me when I was there and I didn't feel welcomed home. It has hurt me for a long time and I've seen the pain in many other vets over the years and it is time for healing, time for me to be healed."

A burst of applause and cheering rang out through the group! People from the welcome team rushed towards me and held out their hands and touched me and whispered "Welcome Home. We're so glad you are back. We missed you. Thank you for being there for the rest of us."

Sky ran over to the piano and started playing parade music like "God Bless America." I, too, was overcome with emotion. Tears began to stream down my cheeks. I dropped to my knees. I could hardly walk. It was like time stood still. It was such a powerful feeling. I'll never forget it!

Every time I would get back up and walk farther into the group, more people would bless me and hold me and welcome me. Sky said, "You are coming home. You are being loved and welcomed." It touched me to the core of my soul. Every cell of my body reacted to that experience.

As I walked through the group, I was shaking, but I could literally feel the pain leaving my body. The anvil I was carrying for so many years was being lifted from my shoulders. The hurt was disappearing as I was being held in the arms of love. I could feel the welcoming that I wanted so much from my country, and I chose to receive it and receive it I did!

I could see the tears on the faces of those people blessing me, and I knew that their love and support were real. It was the greatest healing that I've ever received in my life.

Many people came up to me after the workshop and told me stories about their loved ones' experiences in Vietnam and the difficulties they faced when returning home. These fathers, mothers, and spouses of Vietnam vets also had a need for healing, forgiveness, and understanding. They were grateful for the experience of welcoming me because I represented their loved ones, who also needed to be welcomed home by their country. And so these other participants needed to welcome me as much as I needed to be welcomed by them!

I never knew why I was in Vietnam, and now I have a purpose for having been there—to help support others to remember that it is never, never, *never* too late to be blessed, no matter what we are holding on to, no matter what the circumstance is.

It is never too late to be welcomed home, to be loved, to be supported, to heal old wounds and memories. It is never too late! Don't ever forget that. How do I know? Because it happened to me. And if I can touch anyone's heart from this moment on and help them to remember that, then I will.

I thank God. I thank the vets. I thank Sky St. John. I thank Elisabeth Kübler-Ross for doing this wondrous thing that needed to be done for so many years. God bless them. God bless all of the vets. And God bless you.

This is such a heartwarming story, and it says so much about how wonderful life can be when we simply pay attention to little things that we do and say and express to each other. These are not little things at all, but very big things in the life of the soul.

I hope that I will never allow anyone to feel unwelcome in my space, and I hope that you will never do that either.

From the beginning of time, all that any of us ever really wanted is to love and be loved. And from the beginning of time, all we have done as a society is make it virtually impossible to experience that.

We have created all manner of religious restrictions, tribal taboos, societal strategies, group guidelines, neighborhood norms, borderline barriers, laws, policies, rules, and regulations telling us who, when, where, how, and why we may love, and who, when, where, how, and why we may not.

Unfortunately, the second list is longer than the first.

We have placed judgment before acceptance, condemnation before compassion, retribution before forgiveness, and limitation before freedom in the fashioning of the experience that we have called human love. In one word, we have made love conditional, and with that decision rendered it utterly bereft of meaning, a complete counterfeit, not real love at all.

Yet it is not too late—it is never to late—for our hearts to be opened, and for us to melt into the experience of genuine love given and received. We do this when we bless each other.

This is what happened to David Hiller in the experience he related here. The group blessed David and, itself, felt blessed. That is what always happens, for blessing is the completion of The Circle of Love.

Blessing becomes the natural thing to do when we come to know at last Who We Really Are. Says *Friendship with God*:

> In the moment of your total knowing (which moment could come upon you at any time), you, too, will feel as I do always: totally joyful, loving, accepting, blessing, and grateful. These are the Five Attitudes of God, and . . . the application of these attitudes in your life now can, and will, bring you to Godliness.

Again, please let me say, it is never too late to receive such a blessing and never, *ever* too late to offer it. Even if our hearts are healed in the very last moment of our lives, an entire life can be made to feel worthwhile.

When we are blessed, we feel accepted, we feel welcome. I am so excited to have the "coming home" process described so beautifully and so movingly, in this book, by David Hiller. Now it can move from Elisabeth Kübler-Ross to Sky St. John to David and on out to you—to any of you who may be doing healing work or helping work and who can find ways to adapt it to your program, to your activity, to your particular expression in the world. And do not worry about plagiarism. No one will be angry with you for "stealing" the idea. *They want you to.*

Why? Because now is the time for healing on a grand scale of all people who have felt unwelcome anywhere. I have been asked by people all over the world to bring them the message of *Conversations with God.* From Oslo to Croatia, Copenhagen to Johannesburg, Toronto to Tokyo, the desire for love, the quest for truth, the thirst for understanding, the striving for healing, and the desire for a deeper happiness is palpable.

I have *felt* it in the air at the ruins of Machu Picchu, and at the Vatican in Rome. I have stood on the Great Wall of China and at the Demilitarized Zone still separating, after fifty years, North and South Korea, and everywhere—*everywhere*—it is the same: a hunger for peace and harmony and oneness, and an end, at last, to all that divides us and causes us conflict.

Even though our collective minds still cannot get past their judgments, nor devise a way to set their prejudices and their angers and their imagined needs aside, our combined hearts have no trouble moving to a place where they can agree: people of differing beliefs or cultures, of differing skin color or sexual preference, of differing religions or political persuasions, are truly at their core the same. And while they have all been made to feel unholy and wholly unacceptable at one time or another, in one place or another, in one way or another, there should be *no time* and *no place* and *no way* in which intolerance causes human beings to feel unwelcome—much less, in danger. Not if we are who we say we are. Not if we lay claim to being the most highly evolved creatures on the planet, much less in the universe.

So our challenge now, as we move into the first decade of the twenty-first century, is to increase our openness to new ideas, to new possibilities, and to new ways of understanding each other and God—and God's many gifts.

Including . . .

16

The Gift of Prophecy

Monique Rosales awoke one morning with tears streaming down her face. She had dreamed that her dear mother
had died.

This dream would have been unsettling enough, but for
Monique it was doubly impactful. Many of her dreams had
been fulfilled in the past—including one in which she experienced a reunion with a man she had loved for thirteen
years but hadn't seen for nearly six—and so she knew right
away that she had to call and check on things.

"Mom? Are you okay this morning?" Monique tried to
sound casual through her feelings, a now-familiar mixture of
dread and awe. Why did she have this ability to dream what
would happen in the future? *I don't know if it's a blessing or
a curse*, she thought ruefully.

"Of course, dear, why do you ask?" Her mother was
aware of Monique's strange abilities, of course. So she, too,
was unsettled. She hung up wondering about the meaning of
the dream; usually her daughter's intuition was right on.

The next night, Monique had a second dream like the

first. This time she didn't call her mother, because she didn't want to really upset her with the news that now two dreams had foretold death. Monique just kept it to herself, and worried, and wondered.

Two months later, the mystery was solved. Monique's mother was diagnosed with renal cancer of her left kidney—terminal.

"My God, honey, you were right," her mother had said. Now Monique felt almost guilty about her "gift."

"Oh, Mom, I'm so sorry . . . "

"Dear, it's not your fault. You only saw what was coming. If anything, it made the news of all this less shocking. Please don't feel bad."

Monique nursed her mother during her illness, praying that God would grant them both the strength to bear this painful loss. After just a few months her mom was gone.

Unable to shake free of her deep sadness, Monique spent night after night tossing and turning. It didn't make it easier on *her* that she had these dreams. The next time she has a dream like that about someone she loves, she thought, she'll be mourning not only after their death, but before.

"God, why can't I have a GOOD vision?" she asked plaintively.

And then she did. Her mother appeared to Monique one night in a dream. "I am happy and healthy," she seemed to say. Monique began sleeping easier.

A few years later, Monique was living in Germany and her mother visited her in a dream once again. "You need to be examined by a doctor, Monique," her mom told her. "You have three cysts near your ovaries."

"Will I die, Mama?" Monique asked.

"No, do not worry. But see a doctor right away," she answered.

Even though she'd been reassured, Monique awoke in a panic. She spoke German badly, and so she called an

English-speaking friend to help get her a doctor's appointment. The hours went by slowly until the scheduled day arrived.

As she was being examined, Monique tried to explain to the physician what her mother had told her. He said to her as he peered at the ultrasound screen, "Your mother is right. This is incredible. Where does she live?"

"In heaven," Monique answered.

"How gifted you have been!" said the doctor, and he picked up the phone to schedule surgery within the week.

Three days before going into the hospital, Monique meditated for six hours straight in absolute prayer. She was ready. As she packed her bag for her hospital stay, Monique continued to pray. She was afraid, despite the assurances her mother had given her. She was alone, and she spoke so little German. But, trusting in God, she made her way to the examination room, where one last ultrasound would be performed before the surgery, to make certain of the exact location of the cysts.

The doctor began the ultrasound, but very soon another doctor was called into the examination room. They seemed to be arguing and appeared to be unclear about something having to do with the test. A third doctor was called in. If Monique was nervous beforehand, now she was beside herself. What could be the matter? Had something gone wrong? She lay on the table near panic. Her heart was beating so fast! If only she spoke enough German to ask them what was happening.

Then Monique heard a voice inside her head. It was her mother.

You will be fine, Monique. God has heard your prayer. Trust God to keep you in His love.

Monique breathed deeply. When a translator finally came in, she found Monique confused but calm.

"There's been a change in your condition, apparently,"

the translator explained. "The doctors cannot find any evidence of tumors or cysts. They are quite puzzled."

Monique was bewildered. "What?" she asked. "What are you telling me?"

Indeed, the doctors appeared to be stunned with the test results, explaining through the interpreter, "Normally there would have been at least a trace of a cyst; we are unable to find any indication that you have been ill at all. The cysts appear to be completely gone."

From that moment on, Monique has given thanks for the miracles in her life—including the miracle of her very special gift of being able to receive—and send—important messages to the Greater Realm. She prays that she is using her gift of prophecy in a way that can assist others. And, most of all, she thanks her mother for continuing to be with her and watch over her.

Whenever we hear of people having experiences like this, demonstrating abilities like this, our minds want to know: Is there really such a thing as being psychic? Says *Conversations with God, Book 1*:

> There is such a thing as being psychic. You are that. Everyone is that. There is not a person who does not have what you call psychic ability, there are only people who do not use it.
>
> Using psychic ability is nothing more than using your sixth sense.

But Monique says she received not just psychic "hits"—insights or visions about a future event—but also, *direct communications* from her mother, one when Monique was still reeling from her mom's death, and the other, years later, when her mother came to warn her. Is *this* possible?

From *CWG, Book 3*:

You are talking about communication with spirits. Yes, such communication is possible.

Loved ones are never far from you, never more than a thought away, and will always be there if you need them, ready with counsel or comfort or advice.

If there is a high level of stress on your part about a loved one being "okay," they will send you a sign, a signal, a little "message" that will allow you to know everything's fine. You won't even have to call them, because souls who loved you in this life are drawn to you, pulled to you, fly to you, the moment they sense the slightest trouble or disturbance in your auric field.

. . . you will feel their comforting presence if you are really open to them.

When we understand that Monique's story is not unusual, but that, in fact, it has happened, *and is happening right now*, to many thousands of people, then we will be ready to make that quantum leap for which all of humanity is longing; that leap into tomorrow, when we will recreate ourselves as New Humans.

There are Masters now waking this planet who have reached this level. They have been outcasts in many places and among many people, for their views shake up the status quo, cause us to reexamine ourselves, present us with a startlingly clear view of what we are doing to each other—and how we can stop it, if we merely come to know and accept Who We Really Are.

It is time now to end our separation from each other. We must "welcome home" those who reveal our own magnificence to us. In the past we have mocked them, criticized them, shunned them—and even crucified them. Now we are invited to come to a place of acknowledgment that the gift of insight and wisdom and, yes, even of prophecy, is *common*.

As is . . .

17

The Gift of Healing

We've met Bill Tucker, who lives just outside Milwaukee, Wisconsin, before in this book, in chapter 2. He was the unbelieving real estate office manager whose mouth dropped open in astonishment at each step along the way as Mr. and Mrs. Johnson's miracle unfolded. Bill told me that his life has been literally filled with miracles since that day, and when he described another of them—a startling and powerful story—I could not resist including it too, in this collection, because it illustrates very dramatically a point around which this book revolves:

There *are* things we don't know about, there *is* a direct connection between humans and the Divine, and experiences of this connection are more commonplace than most of society has been acknowledging.

Just as with *Conversations with God* I hoped to shatter, at last, the illusion that God no longer talks directly to human beings, with this book I hope to make it clear that *the extraordinary is commonplace.*

Once we "get" that, we will get that our entire take

about life on this planet has been inaccurate, askew, and incomplete at best. Then we'll start looking, in earnest, for the *real* story.

Those who have a deep investment in our limited and lack-filled lives continuing just the way they have been may have a little difficulty with this. On the other hand, people who are ready now for our collective emergence as New Humans in a new society will welcome these evidences of our readiness and our ability to cocreate that experience.

So now I want to give the floor to Bill Tucker, who has a second interesting story to tell, this one in his own words. . . .

On a cold day in February of 1990, my mother called me from St. Mary's Hospital in Milwaukee.

"You have to get over here to the hospital right away!" she pleaded.

"What's the problem?" I asked.

"Your father was feeling poorly, so I brought him into the emergency room," she cried into the telephone, "and they refuse to talk to me without you here!"

I jumped in my car and sped over to St. Mary's. They sent me down to the Oncology Department. At the time, I didn't know that *oncology* was the cancer ward. My mother took me to the doctor, and I asked him why he wouldn't talk to her.

"Because I have very bad news, and I wanted a family member here for her support."

"Okay," I said, "what's the problem?"

"Put your arms around your mother's shoulders and hold her tight," he said, and I did so. "Your father is dying of cancer . . . and we can do nothing for him." At that my mother screamed, "Oh, God, noooo," and began to pass out. I held her up.

"Isn't there *something* you can do, doctor?" my mother pleaded.

"I'm sorry, but he's been smoking for over fifty years, and eighty percent of both lungs are gone. We can't radiate because the amount of radiation and the area we'd have to cover would kill off all of his other vital organs. Moreover, we can't give chemotherapy because, again, the amount of chemo would most likely kill him, and all we'd accomplish is to make him sick and miserable for his final days. And we can't operate because we'd have to remove both lungs entirely, and he'd have nothing left to breathe with."

My mother was anxious now, looking for any ray of hope. "How much longer does he have?"

The doctor hesitated, then said slowly, "He won't see six months. . . ." and nodded to me to hold my mother once again. I understood that more bad news was coming.

"Doctor," my mother pleaded once again, "we have been planning a vacation to Florida for July. Will he be able to go?"

"I don't think you understand," he said. "Your husband may not see July."

My mother turned to me wide-eyed as if confused by what she was hearing. "What is he saying, Bill?"

"The doctor is trying to tell you as gently as possible, Mom, that Dad is going to die a whole lot sooner than six months." At this she moaned again and, slumping to the floor, actually did faint in my arms. Smelling salts brought her around.

Visibly shaking, she said, "Please, doctor. Just say it. How much longer does he have?" I nodded that it was okay to tell her.

"Well . . . it's impossible to predict . . . of course . . . "— at this I rolled my eyes—"but I don't think he will still be with us three weeks from now." Then the doctor hurriedly added, "But we can give him something for the pain. We'll probably administer radiation, too, but it won't be enough to make a difference in his life span. It will only make him more comfortable."

At that, my mother turned to me and said, "I know that you have a special relationship with God. Son, you must save your father!"

"Hey, Mom," I said. "I'm not Jesus Christ! What can I do?"

"Do you think I don't know about the miracles you've had in your life? I know how your daughter came back from total paralysis in miraculous time," she said. "And I know about all that money you've gotten through prayer.

"Now," she insisted, "you *must* cure your father!"

That's when I made a decision. My mother was right, of course, about my daughter. She did come back from near total paralysis—and I was the one who said she would. She was right about the money, too. I once asked God to give me a million dollars, free and clear, in a specific fourteen-day period. On the fourteenth day, a bank gave me one million dollars as an investment in a business idea I had.

I told everyone that this, too, was going to happen. "God never fails," I'd said.

So now, standing there in the hospital, I knew that it was once again time (you should excuse the expression) to put my money where my mouth is.

I turned to the doctor and said, "Okay. My father is all cured now. He won't die. His cancer is gone."

I'm sure that this sounded flip, but I really wasn't *being* flip. I was being quite sincere. Still, the doctor stared at me, bug-eyed, his mouth dropping open, as if I was crazy. "Denial isn't going to help matters here, son," he said evenly. "Your father is not going to last out the month."

"Doctor, you may have no idea what you are dealing with here, but I'm telling you, my father is cured of his cancer."

With that, my mother and I left the hospital.

I put the matter out of my mind. Since it was a "done deal," I had no reason to think about it, ask again, or "worry" about whether it would come true or not. I *knew* the miracle had already taken place, whether any of us could see the physical evidence of it or not.

They gave my father some radiation . . . actually, surprisingly little, I thought . . . a shot every six weeks for a couple of months. He lingered on. It might be more descriptive to say that he "limped along." Nevertheless, in July, with my father admittedly still pretty sick, my parents went on their Florida vacation!

In October, being a commander in the naval reserve, I was recalled to active duty with the navy for Operation Desert Shield, the precursor to Desert Storm. The Navy sent me to Chicago to fill in for another commander who was sent to Saudi Arabia.

At the end of February 1991, just after the five-day ground war ended, I got a phone call at my navy office. It was my father's oncologist.

"Commander Tucker . . . from Milwaukee?" he asked hesitantly.

"Yes, this is Bill Tucker," I responded.

"Thank God! I've been calling all over the navy trying to track you down!" he said. "You're not going to believe this but . . . "

"Of course I will, doctor," I said before he could finish.

"No, no, listen! You're not going to believe this, but your father is . . . his cancer is all gone!"

"Of course it is," I replied.

"No, no, I mean he's cured! It's a miracle!" He rushed the words out.

"Where have you been?" I asked him. "That happened a year ago last February, there at the hospital."

"What?" he asked, "I don't follow. . . ."

"Doctor, what you have just experienced *is* a miracle. But not in the figurative sense, the way you mean in. In the *literal* sense. Don't you remember when I *told* you that my father was cured?"

"Well, yes, but I mean *this* is the miracle . . . I don't know what else to call it!" he exclaimed, clearly not catching on.

My father went to work regularly for the next seven years. Then one day he fell ill again. We took him back to the hospital, but Columbia Hospital this time, because his doctor worked out of both hospitals and had directed us there.

When we walked in, his doctor rushed up to greet us at the door, and then, standing next to my father with his arm over his shoulders, turned around and announced to all of the staff within hearing distance, "Hey, everybody! Here he is! The Miracle Man!"

The staff, apparently aware of the stories told around the hospital about my father's miraculous cure, broke out in applause. I was glad that these medical professionals were willing to recognize the possibility of a spontaneous miracle, but not so happy that they seemed to be attributing it to me. *There's still a lot of educating to do,* I said to myself.

After completing his physical check of my father, the doctor called me in to consult.

"Well, I'm afraid he's had it this time," he said dejectedly. "This time he's got oat-cell, or commonly called 'small cell,' cancer, and that's the worst kind. It grows very rapidly and is the most resistant to treatment."

"Not to worry, doctor," I said. "He's already cured of it."

The doctor stared at me silently, his eyebrows knitting together in a scowl, pondering my words. Then he said studiously, "I . . . don't . . . think . . . so . . . this . . . time."

I chuckled. "You didn't think so last time, either, Doc. What about God do you think has changed?"

"Hey!" he exclaimed. "I'm not one to knock religion. 'Whatever works' is my motto. But lots of folks have faith, and God doesn't cure them all of cancer."

"Maybe they're not asking God to, doctor. Did you ever think of that? Maybe they're just 'fatalists' and don't bother God with such a request because they believe in 'fate.' Or maybe they ask, but in their heart they doubt that God will come through. That would certainly undo it. But look into my eyes, doctor. Do you see any doubt in me, or in my conviction?"

"Well, we'll just have to wait and see . . . " he trailed off.

"That doesn't sound like a statement of conviction to me, doctor. You see, one has to know—absolutely *know*—in *advance* that the miracle has already happened . . . or it can't happen."

The doctor smiled indulgently. "As you say," he replied quietly.

"Exactly," I smiled back. "Now you've got it!"

The following week the doctor told us that the oat-cell cancer had disappeared, and he watched in awe as we walked out of the hospital.

A week later, Dad was back and the oat-cell cancer had returned. Once again I said my prayer and the following week Dad was declared clear of cancer again.

Then, a few weeks later, it came back yet again. We were becoming regular visitors to Columbia Hospital.

With each returning bout, the cancer seemed to take more and more out of my father. His legs swelled up, so he could hardly get around anymore. His breathing was labored. I could tell that he was miserable.

Over the next seven months, the cancer kept disappearing each time that I said it would, and then returning. I began to feel guilty, as if I were interfering with some greater heavenly plan. I thought, *Am I supposed to be doing this forever? I sure as heck don't want him suffering like this.*

Then it came to me. Something so obvious, I was embarrassed to not have recognized it before.

It wasn't my call.

It wasn't my life.

It wasn't my responsibility.

It was Dad's . . . and God's.

So I said to God, "Please keep him with us as long as possible, but, when it is Your time and his time, please take him, gently."

My father had asked the doctor during his last visit if he could help him stay alive for a few more weeks.

"It's our fiftieth wedding anniversary, Doc. I'd sure like to celebrate it with my sweetheart."

The doctor looked past Dad's shoulder to me, then said, "I'll do my best," and smiled. Three weeks later we all celebrated our parents' fiftieth anniversary.

My father was now housebound and pretty much bedridden, his swollen legs hurting him a great deal. One day soon after their anniversary, while trying to get up to make it to the bathroom, he fell and broke his glasses. I helped him back up to the edge of the bed. He looked at me with the most sorrowful eyes and, crying, said, "Son, it's my time. I don't want to live in pain anymore. Let me die. Please."

I looked heavenward and thought, *We love this man so, but we don't want to keep him beyond his will to live. God, Thy Will be done.*

We had to take him to the hospital then.

He passed away a few hours later.

Like all the wonderful stories being told here, this is a beautiful testimony to God's love, and to the perfection with which life is expressed through all of God's creations.

For everything there is a season, and a time for every

purpose under heaven. A time to be born and a time to die. A time to sow and a time to reap. A time to weep and a time to laugh.

Life is eternal. It has no beginning and it has no end. It has only differing expressions at different points on a cycle that never ends. Death is a fiction and does not really exist, although departure from the body does.

The timing of everyone's departure is always perfect. When Bill's father was initially diagnosed with cancer, it was not time for him to leave. Often, with our limited perception, it is not possible to know that. It may seem as though a person's life with their present body is nearly over, when in truth there may be much more left to be done.

A person who "performs a miracle" is merely a person who has seen clearly, who knows absolutely, what is appropriate to the moment, and who then lays claim to that, who calls it forth.

There are many outcomes we may select for any given moment. This is something that is complicated to fully explain without a deep discussion of the nature of time. Yet space here requires brevity. I will say, then, only that there really is no such thing as time as we know it. That is, time is not something that passes. It is a thing through which *we* pass.

> There is no time but this time. There is no moment but this moment. "Now" is all there is.
>
> —*Conversations with God, Book 2*

The Eternal Moment of Now contains all possibilities. It holds every conceivable outcome. It is like a compact disc holding a computer game. Every conceivable outcome is programmed on the disc. When you play the game, you are not *creating* an outcome, you are simply *choosing* one, through a very intricate process by which you *eliminate all the other possible outcomes, all of which already exist.*

Again, nothing is being *created* in this process. Something is merely being *selected*.

That is exactly what is happening in life.

That is the short of it. A comprehensive explanation of time may be found in large sections of both *Book 2* and *Book 3* of the *Conversations with God* trilogy. It is exciting and intriguing reading. The point here is that it is possible to know, it is possible to almost feel, which outcome is appropriate in any given circumstance and at any given moment during your life. Especially as one grows older (and, therefore, more "used to" feeling life's "vibes"), this begins to become a fairly simple matter.

Now let me explain to you what all this has to do with the story Bill told us, above.

Performing a "miracle" is merely a matter of selecting the *already existing outcome* that is most appropriate to the current experience in the Eternal Moment of Now. It is not a matter of *creating* the outcome, or *producing* it, but simply of *selecting it,* of *choosing it,* and then of clearly and resolutely *announcing your choice.*

This is exactly what Mr. and Mrs. Johnson did when they first encountered Bill Tucker late one evening in a real-estate office many years ago. And their demonstration of this process was something that he never forgot. The Bill Tucker who encountered the doctor at St. Mary's Hospital in Milwaukee years later was not the same man whom the Johnsons encountered. He had changed dramatically. Had he known in that real-estate office what he knows now, he would have said to the Johnsons, when they told him they'd asked God for a house overnight and expected to have one: "I agree with you. I can't think of a reason why not. Let's go get it!"

Today, he would only change one word in that comment. He could change, "I can't think of a reason why not" to, "I *won't* think of a reason why not."

It is the absolute refusal to consider any possibility other than the outcome you have selected that prepares the Field of Possibilities for a miracle. It is the further refusal to judge anything by its appearance that makes the moment ready for magic.

In miracle working, you must be prepared to ignore the evidence of your own eyes, you must close up your ears, and you must be out of your mind. If you are in your head, if you are in your mind, you will think your way right out of the miracle. When you perform miracles, *you do the unthinkable.*

Now, in order to do any this, you must understand it. You must understand that Reality is not what it seems to be. You must be clear that we live in an Alice in Wonderland world, in which we all live by agreement that what is Real is not real, and that what is Not Real is real. And you must understand that, as in Wonderland, everyone is making it all up. But here's what they don't tell you. The one who is the *most convincing* is the one most likely to have it his own way.

Bill Tucker may not have articulated it this way—and Mrs. Johnson most definitely would not have—but this is the process by which both of them have produced miracles in their lives.

When the doctor came to Bill's mother and told her that her husband would not "be with us three weeks from now," that sounded very convincing. And so for a moment there it looked as though the doctor was going to get to say what was real and what was not real. But Bill's mom had seen Bill in action before, and so she quickly turned to him and said, "Do something!"

Bill, realizing the truth of the situation (which is that the others didn't necessarily have to be the ones to decide what is real and what is not real), simply chose something else. He selected a different outcome. And he ignored all appearances in doing so. He paid no attention to what he saw, what he heard, or even what his "rational mind" might have thought.

Bill understood that *all* possibilities exist in the Eternal Moment of Now, that absolutely *no* possibility was ruled out, and that all he had to do was announce the outcome of his choice.

His job was not to create an outcome, but simply to choose one of the many that had already been created, and to declare it.

And what made him choose one outcome over another?

"For everything there is a season, and a time for every purpose under heaven."

I believe that Bill, at some very high, perhaps superconscious, level, felt the vibrations of the moment and found an outcome of similar vibe. He picked one that matched. He called forth an experience that was appropriate to the moment. That is, one that was in harmony with all that was going on.

Then, he held onto that choice. He called it forth deliberately, he boldly announced and declared it, and then changed his perspective to eliminate any other point of view on the matter.

Remember, perspective is everything.

Says *CWG, Book 3*:

> Assume a different perspective and you have a different thought about everything. In this way you have learned to control your thought, and, in the creation of your experience, controlled thought is everything.
>
> Some people call this constant prayer.

Years later, when his father fell ill again, this time repeatedly, even after Bill continued to select other outcomes, Bill again went inside and felt the vibration. It was then that he was sensitive enough to realize that his father was vibrating at a different frequency, and that the outcome Bill kept selecting was not in harmony with his dad's.

Again, this may not be the way that Bill would talk about it. (Or that anyone else would talk about it, for that matter!) But I believe that this is, at its basis, exactly what happened.

In more traditional religious terms, Bill might say that he "asked God" what to do, and then gave up on the need to find an answer, surrendering instead to "God's will."

Traditional religion also says that, where miracles are concerned, the more people you can get praying for one, the better the chances are that one will occur. I think this is very true. *CWG, Book 1* addresses this directly:

> Large communities or congregations often find miracle-producing power in combined thinking (or what some people call common prayer).
> And it must be made clear that even individuals, if their thought (prayer, hope, wish, dream, fear) is amazingly strong, can, in and of themselves, produce such results.

Mrs. Johnson sure showed Bill Tucker what an amazingly strong prayer can do, and Bill's whole life changed out of that. Bill decided then and there that he could do what Mrs. Johnson could do, and he was right.

So can all of us. When we begin to understand how life works, we, too, have access to what my friend Deepak Chopra calls the Field of Infinite Possibilities. Deepak was once asked, "Do we have free will, or is life predestined?" He replied, "It is both, depending on your level of consciousness."

He is right. Consciousness produces perspective. Perspective produces experience. That's how you affect the vibe.

Conversations with God says that "all of life is vibration." I have actually seen this vibration, affecting the very fabric of life. I have watched it pulsate particles of pure energy at the sub-molecular level. So God didn't have to say much to convince me.

Now, if all of life is energy, vibrating (and it is), then amazing things can be done by simply cultivating the ability to "pick up the vibe." *This is what "psychics" do. This is what "healers" do. And this is something we can all do.*

Train yourself to listen to the vibrations of life.

First, you may have to train yourself, train your "receiving instrument" (your body and your mind), to be quiet. If you are not used to being quiet for long periods, to doing nothing but opening yourself to the moment, you may want to take a class in meditation, or read up on it in any one of a hundred books.

Once you've learned to quiet your mind, you'll have opened a channel to the Divine. You'll soon be feeling more sensitive to the vibration of everything. Certain foods will carry a vibe, heavy or light, and you will find yourself making diet choices based on how "in sync" your internal, personal vibe feels with the vibe of that certain food at that particular moment. Likewise, clothes. And, yes, people.

And then, ultimately, the whole *gestalt*. You'll start feeling the vibes of the entire circumstance you find yourself in. And, as you reach in and reach out, you'll start feeling the vibes of the entire circumstance that other people are finding *them*selves in. And if they have not yet learned to get quiet with *them*selves, you may actually feel the vibes of their circumstance *better than they do.*

This is when others will say that you're "psychic." All you've done is pick up the vibration of a selection that someone in the room has made, out of the infinite Field of Possibilities. That's all that any psychic does. That's all—at a much higher level—that spiritual masters do.

That's all, but it's plenty. Because if you can train yourself to pick up on information like that, you've got an incredibly valuable new tool to use in the fashioning of your *own* experience.

Yet sometimes this illusory world creates too much "interference" for us to easily pick up on the vibe, for us to know what's going on, what's appropriate to the moment.

That's when we have to rely on larger, gross-motor skills to make our way through life. It's tough that way. We have to move around very heavy, dense energy (namely, our bodies) a lot more. Life may be giving us too much static, and our "fine tuning" is out of whack, so we're not as clear as Bill Tucker was when he went inside and asked what he should do about his father.

If only we could know what to do! C'mon God, *give us a sign*, we say. But do we think God is actually going to do that? I mean, the monarch butterfly lighting on Susan Tooke's hand was a coincidence, right? God doesn't really "give us a sign" on command!

. . . or *does* She. . . .

18

A "Grand" Sign Indeed

Four years ago, Susan made the decision to wage war with her alcoholism. She was tired of hurting others . . . and herself. The excessive drinking had taken its toll in every area of her life. She was sick, scared, depressed, overweight, and very, very broke. She had a huge debt load, an apartment on which she was paying much too high a rent, and a very modest salary. There was one good thing, however. It had been six weeks since she'd had a drink.

Susan had recently joined Alcoholics Anonymous. Her sponsor was a wonderful lady who was always there when she needed her. Susan was attending meetings regularly and had made a conscious decision to let God manage the nightmare that had been her life for the past few years. She felt that it was now time to trust something greater than herself. It was the only way she was going to beat this.

On this particular Friday afternoon, Susan was making her way to the ATM on the corner to withdraw her last $70 in the world. *Eight days until payday,* she noted despairingly. With this $70 she had to buy groceries and cigarettes, and pay her bus fare.

With a lump in her throat, and despondent about there not being any other options, Susan pressed the right buttons, grabbed the cash from the slot, and stuffed the money into her wallet. Then she headed off to Baskin-Robbins. Ice cream had become her new addiction. Maybe it would help her forget her troubles for a few moments.

"I'll have a double scoop of Jamoca Almond Fudge," Susan told the girl behind the counter. Maybe this would be her dinner, she thought.

"That'll be $2.75," the clerk said, handing her the delicious-looking cone, piled high.

Susan opened her wallet, fingering past the three $20 bills to find the $10 she knew was in there. Only, there weren't three $20s. There were just two . . . along with a $10 bill.

And a thousand-dollar bill.

Susan's heart stopped. Had she seen that right?

The girl behind the counter repeated, "$2.75, please," becoming a little impatient.

Susan looked up at her with a blank stare. She was trying to catch her breath. "Uh, sure. Sorry." She pulled out the $10 bill and handed it over. The girl went off to make change.

The bank machine had given her a $1,000 bill instead of a twenty! Susan was stunned. She could hardly believe her incredible good luck! As soon as the girl returned with her change, Susan turned abruptly and scurried out of the store, throwing the cone in the garbage. Her appetite was suddenly gone.

Although Susan knew that it was . . . well, wrong . . . a part of her began thinking about keeping the money. *I could pay off the phone bill*, she thought. *Or buy a new coat for the winter, or make those overdue credit card payments.*

Another part of her said, the money is not yours, it wouldn't be honest to keep it; and your sobriety depends upon honesty.

Susan had agreed to meet with her sponsor and go to a meeting with her that very night. She began walking the eight or nine blocks to the sponsor's house, all along the way arguing with herself. She knew that if she talked to her sponsor about the money, she would be obliged to return it. She also knew that if she decided to not tell her sponsor, she would end up keeping the money, and lying.

Susan didn't want to lie . . . but she also didn't want to give back the money. She really, really needed it. *Couldn't this just be considered a gift from the universe?* She was trying really hard to justify keeping the windfall.

Oh, God . . . what should I do? she asked inside her head. *Tell me what to do. Give me a sign*, she pleaded.

By the time Susan had reached her sponsor's house, it was clear to her. Without the support of her sponsor, she knew she couldn't make it. She had to tell.

They sat on the porch steps looking out at the street. The light in the sky was dimming. Susan unfolded her story. She was even honest about the thoughts that she had been having about keeping the money, and her struggle with that.

When she was through, her sponsor said quietly, "Well, Susan, that's quite a dilemma."

Susan nodded sadly.

"A thousand dollars could really help you financially right now," her sponsor went on.

"No kidding," Susan agreed. "But keeping it will also create another reason for me to feel guilty in my life. I already have plenty of those."

"Will it?" her sponsor asked.

Susan said nothing. For a while they just sat there, watching the stars becoming visible in the night sky. Then Susan broke the silence.

"I'm going to give the money back. It's the right thing to do, isn't it?" As soon as she asked the question, she began second-guessing herself. "I mean, it is the only thing to do, right? Oh, if only God would give me a sign, then I'd know!"

She really could use a confirming signal from the universe right about now.

Just then Susan's sponsor looked down from the sky to the yard and saw a small object. She went to it, picked it up, and smiled broadly.

"Here's your sign."

She handed Susan a small, shiny object.

"Here's your $1,000."

It was a tiny key chain . . . a miniature replica of a thousand-dollar bill! Susan caught her breath. It was a little banged up, and who knows where it had come from or how long it had been lying there, but it had been there for Susan nonetheless. Her heart skipped a beat for the second time that day. Talk about a sign! she thought, almost laughing out loud. She smiled at her sponsor and slipped the trinket into her pocket.

The next day, she gave back the money.

To this day, that little trinket remains one of her most prized possessions. It serves as a reminder to trust God. She's made her decision to live her life trusting the Universe to bring to her that which is truly best for her.

On that Friday in her life, Susan would have said that $1,000 was exactly what she needed to pull herself out of her financial straits, but that would not have been entirely true. What she really needed was to trust.

Trust God.

Trust others.

And trust herself.

Trust was the long-term solution, she decided that day. And long-term solutions were what Susan was after.

Now, four years later, Susan is financially solvent. She has a better-paying, more secure job, she's lost thirty-five pounds, exercises regularly, has quit smoking and, best of all, she's still sober. She's married to a wonderful, kind, smart, funny man with whom she shares a spiritual life. And God still comes to her in many forms every day.

Oh, and that key chain?

Don't you think it goes everywhere with her?

Okay, okaaaay. So God *does* gives us a sign on command. But the sign cannot tell us the "right" thing to do, it can only make our options known. What "signs" from God often do is startle us into clearing our head. They can make our own values more obvious to us.

CWG says, "Every act is an act of self-definition."

That is what we are doing here. That is what we are up to. We are in the constant act of defining ourselves, and then recreating ourselves anew in our next versions. Hopefully, it's the grandest version of the greatest vision we ever held about who we are. Yet that's not a guarantee.

Susan's dilemma is our dilemma. What is right? What is wrong? Yet in the *With God* series of books the statement is made over and over again that "there is no such thing as right and wrong." These are relative terms, the books say, and human beings have changed their minds about what action is which over and over through the years.

For instance, is it wrong to take money that is not yours? Well, if you're Susan, maybe you think it is. On the other hand, if you're Robin Hood, maybe you think that it isn't. Of course, some would say, Robin Hood stole from the rich and gave to the poor. But isn't keeping money that belongs to a huge corporation (which, you could find a way to argue, has clawed and scraped and cheated its way to the top) and giving it to the poor person called "you" pretty much the same thing? Does the poor person have to be someone else to make stealing okay?

How about the man who steals to feed his family? How about the man who steals to feed himself?

In the end, the thing I think we have an opportunity to notice here is not that Susan "did right" by giving the thousand dollars back, but that her decision to give it back made her feel good about herself. She decided that keeping the money was not the highest version of herself. And she also decided that she wanted to live the highest version. This is not the choice that everyone makes, but it is the choice that she made. This makes her neither better nor worse than anyone else. It simply makes her Susan.

When she received her sign from God, that sign didn't say anything. It didn't say give the money back and it didn't say, keep it, you deserve it, this is a gift from the heavens. It said neither one thing nor the other.

When Susan received her sign, she *read into it* the meaning *that she put there.* She decided what her highest version was and she lived it, even though it may not have been the easier path. But that feeling, the feeling of being the best that she valued herself to be, is what led her to feel even better about herself, and that, in turn, led to making more healthy choices. (Healthy choices are defined as choices that make you feel good about yourself.) And those choices are what produced wonderful long-term outcomes.

Signs from God are wonderful. As with all the other experiences related in this book, they are also very common.

Sometimes, God's signs are hard to spot.

And sometimes, they're pretty darn hard to miss. . . .

19

It's Music to His Ears

Mark Fitchpatrick had been tossing and turning all night, moving in and out of a fitful sleep. It was no use. He reached for the lamp and blinked as light flooded the room, his tired eyes falling on the book on the bedside table where he had put it down only an hour ago.

Damned book, he grumbled inwardly. *Why am I letting this stuff get to me?* He fluffed his pillow and sat up. *I might as well finish it. I can't get it off my mind anyway.*

This book had been a gift to Mark from one of his friends, who thought he might enjoy reading it. Mark had always had a spiritual life, but the hellfire-and-damnation doctrine he had been taught in the church of his childhood had seemed like a half-truth to him at best, and an outright lie at worst. Now moving into his fifth decade on the planet, Mark had become interested in seeking a different point of view about God, one more closely aligned with his own heart. This book, *Conversations with God,* seemed to be articulating it for him. More than that, it seemed to be satisfying something deep in his soul.

That God loves us unconditionally, *really* unconditionally—meaning that God doesn't judge and doesn't punish—was a concept that made sense to Mark. That we create exactly the conditions in our lives in which we can know who we really are, as human beings and as spiritual beings, was an idea that resonated with Mark's way of viewing his own life.

Still, it was all so . . . well, hard to accept intellectually. The ideas presented to him in his formative years had certainly taken hold.

How can I possibly believe this is true? Mark wrestled with his thoughts in his dreams. *Everything I've ever been told . . . in church, at home, at school . . . seems to be the opposite of this message.*

He wondered, *Is it possible that this could all be the overactive imagination of a clever writer, or worse, a literary contrivance to sell books?*

Somehow, though, Mark knew in his heart that it didn't really matter. The point here was to look at God and who God is, or could be, to Mark, personally.

I've known all this my entire life, he kept saying over and over in his mind. *There's nothing in this book I can't agree with.* Nonetheless, Mark couldn't seem to take that final step that would allow him to conquer his last twinge of doubt.

Deciding once again to try to get some sleep, Mark turned off the light. As he was drifting off, the mental argument continued. Even as he drifted in and out of wakefulness, Mark was asking the question over and over, *Is this real?* And somehow he seemed to be answering himself. Or was he *receiving* answers? It was hard to tell.

Throughout the night, Mark was aware of this conversation going on with someone, or some thing. At one point, becoming momentarily very lucid, he even heard his mind say, point blank, *I want this to be real. Give me a sign that this is all real.*

It was then that a clear answer came. A loud voice boomed into Mark's consciousness, saying, *I give you signs every day. Do you not listen? I have given you music; I have given you rocks and trees. Do you not hear my voice when a bird sings and the grass rustles? What more do you need?*

Mark sat bolt upright. The sun was streaming in the window. Looking around his bright room, he realized that morning had finally arrived. As those last words of his dream continued to echo in his head, the refrain of an old Baptist hymn began to play in his mind. Mark started to hum as he threw back the covers . . .

This is my Father's world
And to my listening ears
All nature sings
And round me rings
The music of the spheres.

This is my Father's world
I rest me in the thought
Of rocks and trees, of skies and seas;
His hand the wonders wrought.

This is my Father's world
He shines in all that's fair;
In the rustling grass I hear Him pass,
He speaks to me everywhere.

All of a sudden it hit him. He stopped in his tracks. That song . . . why, it was the very message he'd been given in his dream! The lyrics of the hymn going round and round in his head were the very words that had been spoken to him in the night, the answer to his prayer for a sign.

Now, that's interesting, Mark mused as he began to get ready for church. It was Sunday morning, and it was Mark's habit to go to the early service at the Methodist church he had been attending lately.

As he dressed, he continued to hum the tune. He felt strangely rested, even after reading late into the night and getting very little sleep. He also felt strangely calm, as if the argument in his head had somehow been resolved.

He noticed the time.

Hey, Mark, get a move on or you're going to be late.

He fumbled for his keys in his coat pocket, slamming the door behind him.

As he backed his car out of the garage, the thought came that he could drown out the tune in his head by turning on the car radio. He reached across to turn it on. At once, blaring from the speaker, was a sweet choir singing, "This is my father's world, and to my listening ears . . . "

Mark slammed on the brakes and stared at the radio. *Whaaaat?* He couldn't believe what he was hearing! *What IS this?* he asked himself. Looking closer, he noticed that the radio was tuned to a station to which he never listened. It was some FM music station, and Mark always kept the radio tuned to AM talk radio.

Who had changed the channel? And, more to the point, how had this particular song come on at this particular moment? Mark was flabbergasted.

Okay, God. I hear you. I've gotten my sign. You don't have to hit me over the head with it.

Tears began to form at the corners of Mark's eyes. *Well, ask and you shall receive,* he conceded.

It was a beautiful day in Atlanta. Spring comes early and is always welcome after the months of cold and rain. The dogwoods were beginning to bloom here and there and an occasional daffodil was poking out of the ground. It was the kind of day that made one think of Easter, and new beginnings.

As the church service began, the music minister asked the congregation to stand. Mark noticed, as he always did, the lovely stained-glass window depicting Jesus as a shepherd. The deep red of his robe contrasted with the little white lamb in his arms and at his feet. Mark had always loved this particular portrayal of the aspect of Christ as a gentle protector. It seemed to more closely resemble the Jesus that resided in Mark's own heart.

"Please turn your hymnal to page fifty-nine, our opening song this morning."

The choir led the congregation as the strains of the lovely tune wafted out into the room.

"This is my father's world . . . "

Mark grabbed the back of the pew in front of him! He stood there shaking, his heart pounding. *I get it!* he almost screamed aloud. *Thank you! I get it!*

Mark knew then, without a doubt, that the voice he had been hearing all his life, in his dreams and in his waking world, was the voice of God—a voice reminding him that God is the God of love . . . and of rocks and trees, and skies and seas.

And the very God of his highest imagining.

Coincidence? *Conversations with God* says there's no such thing as coincidence. If we believe that, if we believe that all things happen with a purpose, that all things happen for a reason, then we are already well on our way to fathoming what we have been told is the unfathomable machinery of the universe.

Little things, big things, things in between—all things are God's things, and not a single thing of God's is ever wasted.

Have you every prayed to God on a starry night—really prayed, I mean, prayed *really hard*—and asked God, begged God, "Oh God, if you can hear me now, please, please let me know. *Somehow*, let me know"—only to see, *at that exact moment*, a shooting star?

Have you ever cried out in your heart, "Oh, Mom, I know it was meant to be that you left us when you did. But if only I could know that you're in a good place, that you're okay, and happy! I'd give anything if you could just *come to me now and give me a sign*"—only to have someone walk right past you in the church or the funeral home or wherever you were, *wearing the exact fragrance your mother always wore?*

Now let me ask you a question.

Do you think these things happen by chance?

When you need help of any kind, when your heart is breaking, when your soul is hurting, when you're feeling sadness or depression, shame or guilt or fear, or are in need of any healing, big or small, I promise you, God will be there.

In one manifestation or another, God will be there.

As an Angel, maybe. Or a Guide. Or a Voice. Or your Higher Self.

Or your dog, coming over to lick your hand just when you need comfort.

Or that lady pulling out of the parking spot right in front of the building, just when you desperately need not to be late.

Or a deer that crosses the road, just when you need to simply be reassured that you've really done all that a mother can do. . . .

20

A Mother's Message

The September morning sun danced on the frosty wind-shield as Nancy Hampson drove along Interstate 5 from Seattle to Olympia. She couldn't help but reflect on her life on this day, of all days.

She was taking her youngest daughter off to college.

The car was loaded down with Joanie's books and clothes and a few small pieces of furniture. Nancy looked over at Joanie in the passenger seat next to her. The younger woman was looking straight ahead, hope and wonder painting her face.

Nancy remembered that feeling. It's wonderful to share these moments with your children, understanding them in a way they can never fully realize until they become parents themselves, she thought.

Nancy herself had earned a B.A. degree, many years ago now, but rather than embark on a professional career, she had devoted herself to being a mom. She took a tedious, dead-end job because it allowed her to work at home and be available to her daughters. And now that devotion had paid off—her girls were healthy and happy and starting out with their own lives, their futures bright.

Nancy had anticipated this moment—her final child trundling off to conquer the world. What she hadn't anticipated was the cacophony of emotions sweeping over her, and the many questions swarming around in her thoughts. *Is Joanie ready to be on her own?* Perhaps more poignantly, *Am I ready to be on my own?*

Nancy replayed every happy and not-so-happy memory from Joanie's growing up, stopping to blame herself once again for the two divorces and multiple relocations. *Well,* she sighed, *it's too late for recriminations now. What's done is done.*

Still, she felt herself filling with regret. She took a deep breath.

Turning off the highway onto the quiet, woodsy drive that led to the school, Nancy noticed the leaves of the vine maples just beginning to show a little color. Soon they would be flaming red and golden. She loved this time of year, and this part of the country—the Pacific Northwest—where she'd finally chosen to settle. And right now she should have been feeling peacefully serene, like the countryside itself. But no. She had to send her daughter off today, off on a new adventure, off on the next journey in her own life.

Nancy experienced the inner turmoil that, at a moment like this, only a mother could fully understand.

Perhaps, something moving off to her left caught her eye. Her heart skipped a beat as she braked an abrupt stop. A beautiful doe emerged from the bushes alongside the road, carefully stepping down the bank toward the car and halting only a few inches from them.

As Nancy and Joanie watched transfixed, a tiny fawn ventured tentatively out of the trees and followed her mother. The doe crossed the road first, then paused to let her baby come alongside and catch up with her, protecting her, showing her the way. Then the mother nudged her gently up the slope on the other side. Before disappearing into the woods, the doe turned and gave Nancy a long look.

Nancy looked back.

Something seemed to pass between them.

Something . . . *felt*.

Something *that could only pass between mothers*.

Then the doe turned and disappeared into the forest, behind her little one.

Nancy had not realized how close to weeping she had been, but the gaze of the deer opened something inside her that she had been clenching. Pent-up tears streamed down her face as she realized the perfect gift of that moment. The awesome metaphor for her own inner conflict had unfolded as if it were staged just for her.

Of course she had made mistakes. Of course she had been less than she'd wanted to be as a parent. Many times she had made questionable decisions. But, like the doe, she had guided her little one safely this far, she had tried to protect her, she had shown the way, and now she was here to help her set out on her own path.

Peace and gratitude instantly replaced the turmoil in Nancy's heart. As she wiped her tears and put the car in gear, she whispered "thank you" to God for the glorious teaching. And she inwardly blessed the little fawn, and her Joanie, on their way to the future.

We are on our way to the future, too. We are as beloved offspring, setting off on a new path as we move into this new millennium, beginning to understand things that we could barely comprehend even existed a few short years ago, preparing to take on the largest questions of life, eager to solve the grandest mysteries of the universe.

We have been members of a very young society, you and I. Some might even say, a primitive society. But we are on the verge, at last, of coming to maturation, of growing and discovering and blossoming into our larger selves. We carry with us into our future an extraordinary and enormous potential. We have all the equipment that we need to face our breathtaking tomorrows. We have the technology, and the ingenuity to create even greater technology. We have the insight, and the ability to achieve even greater insight. All we need now is a little nudge. A little push in the right direction.

The time of our emergence is at hand. It is time to cross the road. Time to start up the hill on the other side.

We can do this. We can make it. And it will be all the easier if we know, if we believe, that we have help; that we have a partner, a cocreator, a friend; that God is on our side, blessing us on our journey, showing us the way, giving us a little nudge—and inviting us to nudge each other as well.

These "nudgings" by God are what I have called Moments of Grace.

They come in many forms, often at the oddest times, frequently in the strangest places, always in the perfect way.

Our challenge is not to miss these moments. And further, to pass them on. For one of the best ways to nudge each other is to do what you can do to alter the collective reality, to change our collective mind, to recreate our common experience on this planet.

Right now, society is limited by its present understandings, and those understandings do not always include clarity about the kinds of things that happen, the kinds of energies that swirl, the kinds of relationships with The Divine that are evidenced during Moments of Grace.

Religion tells us on one hand that miracles are possible, and to believe in them. Yet on the other, we are told that miracles are unusual, extraordinary, uncommon. What we have a chance to do is demonstrate that just the opposite is true.

I wish I could one day see a huge billboard in every city

and town with a three-word message that could really change people's minds about how life works:

MIRACLES ARE COMMONPLACE.

Now that's an oxymoron, isn't it? I mean, how can something be a "miracle" if it's something that's happening every day? That's the beauty of the message. It runs counter to the current culture. It says that what is uncommon is common.

That's a message the world would do well to hear right now. It would be nice to know that the extraordinary spiritual events of the Bible and the Koran and the Bhagavad Gita and the Book of Mormon and all the sacred scriptures of all the sacred traditions are not extraordinary at all, *but are happening to all of us, all the time.*

Perhaps it's time to demystify the mystical. Perhaps it's time to bring God down to Earth. For that is where God is. On Earth. As It is in Heaven.

Once we understand and truly know that God is right *here*, right *now*, the space of the Here and Now is wide open to the most extraordinary possibilities.

But history teaches us that the human race will not come to these understandings simply because religion wants it to. These are not truths that will be adopted because they are *taught*. They are truths that will be adopted only after it is demonstrated that they represent, in fact, *the real experience of human beings.* That is why sharing our experiences of God and telling people about our Moments of Grace can be—and is—so impactful. And that is why this book ends with . . .

21

The Invitation

The question that I want this book to ultimately address is not, do a lot of people really experience Moments of Grace? The question is, what do people who experience them do afterward?

Some people brush them aside, write them off, keep quiet about them, even try to forget them. Others, like the folks in this book and many more who wrote to us, share them freely, so that not only they, but people everywhere, may be inspired by them, may learn from them, may come to remember something they've always known. I have an idea that those who do so are helping to heal the world.

Yet why bother to heal the world if—as *Conversations with God* declares—everything is perfect just the way it is?

Well, you know, there is really only one reason to do anything—wear the clothes we wear, drive the car we drive, join the group we join, eat the food we eat, or tell the story we tell—and that is to decide who you are.

Everything we think, say, and do is an expression of that. Everything we select, choose, and place into action is its manifestation. We are in the constant process of recreating ourselves anew in the next version of ourselves.

We are doing this individually and collectively every minute of every day. Some of us are doing it consciously, and some of us are doing it unconsciously.

Awareness is the key. Awareness is everything. If you are aware of what you are doing, and why you are doing it, you can change yourself and change the world. If you are unaware, you can change nothing. Oh, things will change in your life and in your world all right, but you will not have the experience of having had anything to do with that. You will see yourself as an observer. As a passive witness. Perhaps even as a victim.

That is not what you are, but that is what you will think that you are.

This is how it is when you are creating yourself and your world unconsciously. You are doing things, you are putting energy out into the world, *but you have no idea what you are doing.*

On the other hand, if you are aware, if you know and understand that every thought, word, and deed places creative juice into the machinery of the universe, you will experience your life in a totally different way. You will see yourself as George Bailey in the movie *It's a Wonderful Life*, understanding at last that there can be incredible end-of-the-line impact from your in-the-moment choices and actions. You will have stood back from the tapestry to see the beauty of its design, and you will be keenly aware of the interweavings that were required to produce it.

If the world is right now the way you want it to be, if it is a reflection of your highest thought about yourself and about human beings as a species, then there is no reason at all to "heal" anything.

If, on the other hand, you are not satisfied with the way things are, if you see changes that you would like to make in our collective experience, then you might have a reason to tell your story.

For my part, I see us walking around on this planet with a great many false thoughts about ourselves. These are part of the Ten Illusions of Humans that I first mentioned in chapter 8, and which are discussed in great detail in *Communion with God*. The book also explores how we can live *with* these illusions, but not *within* them. Finally, the text reveals how we can all have a direct experience of communion with God, any time we choose.

This is good stuff. This is information that could change the world. But here is the larger point: none of the material in any of the *With God* books would be available to anyone had their author been reluctant to share, to come out into the open, to say amazing things, and to make incredible statements about having had a particular conversation. . . .

I truly do not mean that to be self-congratulatory. I mean it to be an encouragement to all of *you* who have been touched by The Divine in ways that cannot be denied. For if, indeed, the world as you witness it does not present an accurate reflection of your highest thoughts for all of us, *then yours is the opportunity, as was mine, to come forward, to tell your truth, to share your story, and to lift us all up in our Awareness.*

We have a chance now to move to the next level. Or, we can continue to operate on this planet as a primitive culture, imagining ourselves to be separate from God and separate from each other.

The breathtaking futurist and visionary, Barbara Marx Hubbard, in her book *Conscious Evolution*, and in her latest title, *Emergence*, discusses the challenges before us. Barbara says that, for the first time in human history, the members of our species are not merely observing their own evolution, but consciously creating it. We are not only seeing ourselves "becoming," we are *choosing* what we wish to become.

Of course, we have always been doing that. We simply didn't know it. We were not aware of the role we were playing in the evolution of our own species. Mired deep in the Illusion of Ignorance, we imagined that we were just "watching it happen." Now, many of us see that we are *making* it happen.

We are doing this by moving from the place called "effect" to the place called "cause" in the Cause and Effect Paradigm. Yet if more of the human race does not make this shift, we could easily go the way of other once-great civilizations that thought themselves to be hovering on the verge of greatness. They had developed marvelous wonders and extraordinary tools with which to manipulate their worlds, yet their technologies raced ahead of their spiritual understandings, leaving them without a moral compass, without a higher understanding, without any awareness at all of what they were doing, of where they were going and why. They went, therefore, the way of self-annihilation.

Now, once again, our earthly society has come to this same precipice. We are on the brink. We are at the edge. Many of us, individually, can sense it. All of us, collectively, are impacted by it.

We have come to a major crossroad. We can go safely no farther with our limited understanding. We can take one path or the other, but if we do not know why we are taking it, we are gambling with the future of our species.

We must grapple now with larger questions, embrace now larger answers, consider now larger thoughts, imagine now larger possibilities, hold now larger visions.

Our technologies have brought us to the cliff of our comprehension. Are we going to fall, plummeting to our collective death? Or shall we leap from the cliff and fly?

We can clone life forms and are only months away from having the ability to clone humans. We have decoded the human genome. We can do genetic engineering, crossbreed animals, unravel life itself, and put it back together again. On May 4, 2001, the first genetic modification of human babies was reported.

Where is this all leading us? Listen to Francis S. Collins, director of the National Human Genome Research Institute, as quoted by writer Michael Kimmelman in the February 16, 2001, *New York Times*:

"I wouldn't be surprised if in another thirty years that some people will begin to argue, as Stephen Hawking already is, that we ought to take charge of our own evolution and should not be satisfied with our current biological status and should as a species try to improve ourselves."

And I tell you that there will come a time when human beings living a life as we now do—open to what Shakespeare called "the slings and arrows of outrageous fortune," subject to the whims of nature and the accidental confluence of biological events—will be seen not merely as primitive, but as unthinkable.

Conversations with God says that human beings were, in fact, designed to live forever. Or at least, as long as they choose. With the exception of accidents, death is not something that should take anyone when they do not want to go—much less by surprise. An enormous percentage of our human illnesses, our biological discomforts, our systemic misfortunes, are preventable or curable even today. Give us another three decades and they could well *be* completely avoidable. *Then* what?

Then we will have to address, once again and with a completely open mind, the larger questions of life which we approach now only with hesitancy and timidity, wishing to neither blaspheme nor offend. I believe that our answers to those questions will determine how we will use our new technologies and abilities—and whether we produce miracles or debacles.

Yet we must first be willing to even *face* the questions, and not avoid them—or, worse yet, imagine in our hubris that we have already faced them and now have all the answers.

Have we?

Do we already have the answers?

Look at how the world works.

Then decide.

I don't think we have. I think we still have some matters to explore. Here are some of the inquiries I think we must continue to make:

Who and what is God?

What is our true relationship to the Divine?

What is our true relationship to each other?

What is the purpose of Life?

What *is* this thing called Life, and how do we fit into it in a way that makes sense to our soul?

Is there such a thing as the soul?

What is the point of *all of this?*

What we need a little more of on this planet is what Sir John Templeton calls Humility Theology. That is a theology that admits *it does not have all the answers.*

Who or what could cause us to embrace such a theology? Who or what could cause us, as a society, to face these questions anew?

You.

You could.

If you have had experiences such as those you have been reading about in this book, if you have had encounters such as those of Jason and Janice and Denise and Troy and all the others you've met here, then you, too, could turn your personal Moment of Grace into a moment of grace for thousands of others and, ultimately, the entire human race. Because *the sharing of your spiritual experiences will bring into sharper focus the matters that we all ought now, as an evolving society, be addressing.*

Do we really have all the answers about God? Do we really know who God is, and what God wants, and how God wants it? And are we really sure enough about all this *to kill people who do not agree with us?* (And then to say that God has condemned *them* to everlasting damnation?)

Is it possible, just *possible,* that there is something we don't know about all this, the knowing of which could change everything?

Of course it is. And more and more people coming forward and talking about their own "conversations with God" and their own interactions with The Divine is what will cause us all to see that.

So, my friends, it's time to come out of the closet. It's time to raise our hands, to tell our stories, to shout our truth, to reveal our innermost experiences, and let those experiences raise eyebrows. Because raised eyebrows raise questions. Questions about How It All Is that *must be raised* if the human race is to experience what Barbara Marx Hubbard calls "emergence."

Let me tell you about an interesting theory recently placed before us by the extraordinary author-philosopher Jean Houston in her latest book, *Jump Time.* I think it's pertinent here.

It is Ms. Houston's idea that the human race does not evolve slowly over a period of many years, but, rather, remains stagnant for vast periods, and then, in the comparative blink of a cosmic eye, lurches abruptly forward, taking gigantic evolutionary steps virtually overnight. Then, life returns to stasis for another hundred or thousand or million years, until the quiet building up of energies once again—like a dormant volcano erupting—produces Jump Time.

It is Ms. Houston's further theory that we are at Jump Time right now. Evolution, she assesses, is about to make another one of its quantum leaps.

I agree. I see the same thing. Really, I think I have felt it. I have felt it coming on. Many people have. Barbara Marx Hubbard has. Marianne Williamson has. Deepak Chopra has. Many, many people have. Perhaps you have.

Now, to help human beings also make this leap, and not be left behind *by* it, here is what I think we must do. We must share our stories about the sacred things we know, which we have learned in the most sacred moments of life. For it is in these sacred moments, these Moments of Grace, that sacred truths are *made real* for the entire culture. And it is in the *living* of its most *sacred* truths that a culture advances as the universe evolves, and in the *failure* to live those truths that a culture expires.

But let's be clear here. I am not talking about forcing anyone to believe anything. I am not talking about proselytizing or converting or even convincing. I am talking about simply sharing our experience, rather than hiding it. Because we don't wish to expire, but wish to advance.

Let's return to our nights around the campfire, when we told the tales of our heart. That's what I'm inviting us to do. Let's break out the marshmallows and the graham crackers and share our stories, even if they sound a little weird. Perhaps *especially* if they sound a little weird. Isn't that what sitting around the campfire is for?

Our campfire today is the Internet. It is the flame that will shoot high into the sky, with our sharings, like floating embers, carried on the wind to all the wherevers.

The Internet, yes, and, still, good books. Good books, like good nights around the campfire, are always remembered.

And then there is simply good, old-fashioned, in-person sharing—which can bring the feeling of the campfire to wherever it occurs, and so, makes the highest impact of all.

Let's tell each other what is so for us, what is going on with us, what is true about what we have seen and experienced in our lives. Let's tell each other our innermost truth about God, about ourselves, about spirituality, about love, and about all the higher callings of life, the callings that stir the soul, and give us evidence of its existence.

I don't think we're talking to each other nearly enough about these things. We're watching TV and reading the stock quotations and asking, "How 'bout them Dodgers?" We're working our buns off ten and twelve and fourteen hours a day and crawling into bed exhausted and trying to find the flame for a real talk and a deeply meaningful and intimate interaction with the person on the other side of the mattress when we barely have enough fire in the belly to say goodnight.

It has been too long since many people have had a real *discussion* about anything. I'm talking about what Jean Houston calls Deep Dialogue. I'm talking about exposure here. I'm talking about nakedness. Not ego-driven chattering, but experience-sharing, truth-exposing, secret-revealing, mind-opening, heart-expanding *exchanges of soul energy*.

Let's start relating again. Let's begin to really notice our many, many Moments of Grace, and *call them that*, so that we don't *miss* life while we are *living* life.

This is what I call The Invitation.

It comes from the Cosmos, not from me.

It is Life inviting Life to tell Life more about Life.

It we accept The Invitation, it may mean bucking the tide. It may mean sounding a little weird, or being called a little crazy. It may even mean opening ourselves to ridicule.

That is the cost.

That is the price.

That is the tariff for Coming Home.

In Closing . . .

If you would like to share your personal story of a Moment of Grace with the world, and so help *change* the world, send a written account to:

Moments of Grace
Personal Stories
PMB 1144
1257 Siskiyou Blvd.
Ashland, OR 97520

Or you may e-mail it to: momentsofgrace@cwg.cc

Don't worry about having to be a good writer or wonderful at expressing yourself. Just tell your truth. Rita Curtis, our extraordinary editor, will work with you to find the words that will convey exactly what occurred, and how it felt, just as she did with the folks whose stories appeared here.

Not every story that we receive can be used, but those that fit our space and editorial requirements will be eligible to appear in a future *Moments of Grace* book, or in our magazine of the same name. In addition, selected stories will also be edited and posted on our worldwide website: www.momentsofgrace.net.

Here are some guidelines to consider when submitting your story.

- Stories of real-life occurrences in which you feel God or Angels or Guides or a Benevolent Force by whatever name you choose to call it played a crucial role in your life will be considered for use in the Moments of Grace series.

- A story in which we cannot use your real name or city of residence is much less likely to be published.

    This is God in action we are testifying to here, and when people read something that's incredible or hard to believe, some might say, "Outlandish . . . it never happened . . . Neale makes these stories up." Our readers need and want to know that the story is *real*—and what makes it real is that *real people* stand up and say, *Yes, this actually happened to me!* So please give us permission, if you agree, to use your real name (and to edit your story if we need to) when you send it in to us.

    If your story contains information that you do not want others to know about, then you should not submit it. But remember, part of the reason we are having such a challenge in shifting the way our society sees and understands God is because many people who have had really impactful, real-life experiences of God working directly in their life *do not want to tell anyone else about it* for fear of being embarrassed by the details. (I don't have to point out that if I had used that yardstick, none of my books would have been written. . . .)

- A story in which a product or service is being promoted will not be used.

- A story which says that your Moment of Grace was when you picked up *Conversations with God* and that it changed your life will not be used unless the circumstance is unbelievably extraordinary, because overuse of such stories (we receive hundreds) could appear to be self-serving on our part.

I anticipate a huge outpouring of people's personal stories and a huge movement of energy around this. I believe that people all over the world have been waiting for an opportunity to stand up and be counted for God. I see conferences and annual conventions and gatherings of all kinds held by people who have experienced MOGs and want to compare notes with each other. I see interviews being conducted by the media and sincere inquiries being made by churches. I even see lapel buttons and bumper stickers asking: HAVE YOU HAD AN MOG TODAY?

I see an entire world being awakened. And I see you doing this. Not me, but all of *you*. Because you agree that now is the time.

You know, when you think about it, this could be one of the human race's biggest ever . . .

Moments of Grace.

Blessèd be.

Neale Donald Walsch
Ashland, Oregon
February 2001

Appendix

About the people you've come to know here . . .

Chapter 1:

Janice Tooke, 43, lives in Herkimer, New York, holds a B.S. in Psychology and works as an adult protective agent servicing individuals who have chosen to live with the challenges of physical, mental, and developmental differences. She also creates portrait artwork and has illustrated a children's book.

Bill Colson lives in Lehi, Utah, where he is an active member of the Church of Jesus Christ of Latter-Day Saints.

Chapter 2:

William Tucker, 58, decided to become an atheist at age thirteen when he saw a six-year-old child run down by a drunk driver. He's since changed his mind about God because his life has been full of miracles. He is a commander in the naval reserve and lives near Milwaukee, Wisconsin.

Chapter 3:

David A. Daniel, 50, is an author and editor, whose works cover a wide variety of subjects. He is currently working on his new novel, *Down in One*, a golf mystery.

Chapter 4:

Fred Ruth, 64, and his wife, Anne, live in Hamilton, Ohio, where they publish a community newspaper, using the creation skills taught by *CWG*—knowing, being, and experiencing. He never misses an opportunity to discuss the material that has changed his life.

Chapter 5:

Doug Furbush, 53, lives in Alpharetta, Georgia, and is a manufacturing systems consultant for a global company.

Chapter 6:

Carolyn Leffler, 47, lives in Indianapolis and works as a mental health advocate. The loves in her life are her family, friends, books, and photography.

Chapter 7:

Denise Moreland, 49, lives and works in Hawaii. She has created TourTalk–Hawaii Nei, a self-guided audiotape tour of Oahu's sites featuring cultural and spiritual concepts of old and new Hawaii. Also a part-time author and speaker, she is married to her best friend, Mike, and is mother to a blended family of four adult children.

Chapter 8:

Gerry Reid, 61, is a computer software teacher in Whitby, Ontario, Canada, and thanks God every day for his brain injury.

Chapter 9:

Troy Butterworth, 33, works as a computer graphics specialist in Manhattan, where he has been in a 12-Step program for four years. His childhood home was in Texas, and Troy Butterworth is not his real name. He asked us to change his name for this story in deference to his father and his family.

Chapter 10:

Kevin Donka, 40, is a chiropractor with a family health, wellness, and life improvement center in Palatine, Illinois.

Chapter 11:

Maria Endresen, 36, lives in Vancouver, Washington, with her husband and three children. She has taught preschool for the last fourteen years and is now a junior at Concordia University, working toward her degree in education.

Chapter 12:

Jason Gardham, 59, is a schoolteacher in Phoenix, Arizona, working with second graders who speak English as a second language. He believes that, for many of his students, his classroom is their only place of happiness and refuge. This year he received the Excellence in Education award.

Chapter 13:

John Star had his experience nearly forty years ago but figured out how to get back to that place any time he wishes. He now works diligently to save the planet. He chose not to tell us where he lives.

Chapter 14:

Margaret Hiller, 52, is ordained as an interfaith minister and has a master's degree in therapeutic psychology. Since 1979 she has traveled extensively in the U.S. and other countries, facilitating groups in the healing and heart-opening process. She maintains a psychospiritual counseling practice in Ashland, Oregon, and Santa Barbara, California.

Chapter 15:

David Hiller, 52, is an ordained interfaith minister, author, spiritual counselor, and personal empowerment coach and has a master's degree in counseling. He has traveled extensively in the U.S., conducting healing, meditation, and fear-release seminars. He has twenty years of counseling experience working with individuals and groups in their healing process and maintains a private practice of psychospiritual counseling in Ashland, Oregon, and Santa Barbara, California.

Chapter 16:

Monique Rosales, 36, lives in South Bend, Indiana. She was the third of five children, brought up in a Roman Catholic household. She was separated from her family at age twelve while caring for her aunt in Costa Rica. The pain from this separation led to a battle with an eating disorder for eighteen years. She has always had prophetic dreams and visions, and through forgiveness and faith in God, she has been able to find her self-love and compassion in order to help others. She is published in the *Chicago Women's Journal*; her webpage of poetry can be found at http://members.aol.com/msmonique.

Chapter 17:

Bill Tucker's biographical footnote appears above.

Chapter 18:

Susan F. is forty years old and works as an executive secretary near Toronto.

Chapter 19:

Mark Fitchpatrick, 50, is in the wedding business in Atlanta, specializing in flowers and cakes.

Chapter 20:

Nancy Hampson, 40, just returned from a world trip to Thailand, India, and Cambodia, the highlight of which was seeing the Dalai Lama on New Year's Eve and celebrating her birthday. She is embarking on a new career as a technical writer.

About the Editors

Rita Curtis, story editor, works with Neale Donald Walsch and the ReCreation Foundation to bring the message of *Conversations with God* to the world. Besides being story editor of this book, she is the founding managing editor of the *Moments of Grace* magazine. She painstakingly read hundreds of submissions for this book, selected and researched the stories appearing here, and interviewed many of the contributors. She and Neale then cowrote these personal stories, based on her early notes and drafts.

Nancy Fleming-Walsch, book editor, is cofounder and president of ReCreation, the nonprofit foundation for personal growth and spiritual understanding, which is committed to spreading the message of the *With God* series of books around the world. She is owner and editor-in-chief of Walsch Books, an imprint of the Hampton Roads Publishing Company, which publishes books by authors whose work moves forward the message of *Conversations with God* through other voices and articulations. Her review of the first-draft manuscript produced many

improvements, and her suggestions for specific commentaries resulted in much of the material that
appears here.

About the Magazine

If you would like to stay connected with the inspiring and healing energies of this book, you are invited to subscribe to *Moments of Grace*, the magazine, in which will be found many of the personal stories we were unable to fit into this book, plus those that will be sent to us, together with individual commentaries by Neale Donald Walsch. Subscriptions may be obtained by sending your name and mailing address, plus $35 for each yearly subscription, to:

Moments of Grace Magazine
Subscription Dept.
PMB 1144
1257 Siskiyou Blvd.
Ashland, OR 97520

or by calling 1-888-287-9910 and ordering
with your Visa or MasterCard

About the Artist

Elizabeth Hinshaw is a self-taught portrait artist who specializes in charcoal and pastel pencils. For fifteen years she has been showing her art and accepting commissions from corporate and private clients around the world. Elizabeth may be reached at P.O. Box 585, Ashland, OR 97520.

Hampton Roads Publishing Company

. . . for the evolving human spirit

Hampton Roads Publishing Company
publishes books on a variety of subjects including
metaphysics, health, complementary medicine,
visionary fiction, and other related topics.

For a copy of our latest catalog,
call toll-free, 800-766-8009,
or send your name and address to:

Hampton Roads Publishing Company, Inc.
1125 Stoney Ridge Road
Charlottesville, VA 22902
e-mail: hrpc@hrpub.com
www.hrpub.com